Teaching Tools *for* Anthropology Careers

Resources for Instructors and Departments

Editors

Riall Nolan

Irene Greene

Tereza Emilova

Jennifer Studebaker

and Elizabeth K. Briody

ACRN PRESS

ACRN PRESS

https://anthrocareerready.net

ISBN 979-8-9912198-2-2

Printed in the United States of America

How do you prepare anthropology graduates for meaningful careers?

This book contains 37 tools that provide straightforward guidance about career readiness for programs and individual instructors. The tools are intended to complement and enhance your current departmental offerings and are organized into three groups: Moving Your Department Ahead; Building Career Readiness into Your Courses; and Securing Anthropology's Future. They can be used in conjunction with the workbook, *Career Tools for Anthropology*. Put your anthropology to work!

Teaching Tools for Anthropology Careers:

"…is an invaluable resource for educators. It not only provides practical, easy-to-adopt strategies to enhance individual courses, but it also equips departments with actionable frameworks to institutionalize changes. This book helps programs prepare students for successful, meaningful careers."
— **Alejandro Cerrón,** Associate Professor, University of Denver

"…is a fantastic companion to ACRN's *Career Tools for Anthropology* Workbook! It offers departments a comprehensive resource for leveraging anthropological skills with clarity and intentionality."
— **Melissa A. Nelson,** Senior Lecturer, University of North Texas

"…shows how the experiences of anthropologists working across a wide range of careers can be translated into teaching that helps the next generation thrive in an even wider range of careers."
— **Michael Wesch,** Professor and University Distinguished Teaching Scholar, Kansas State University

"…helps professors design career-ready anthropology curricula that build student skills and knowledge. This training teaches students to communicate effectively to employers and diverse audiences how anthropological insight addresses the most pressing problems of today *and* tomorrow."
— **A.J. Faas,** Professor and Graduate Coordinator, San José State University

"...provides exactly what our discipline needs right now—clear, practical, and innovative tools that connect anthropological education to real-world practice, equipping students with the professional skills they need to thrive after college and also shape the future of the discipline."

— **Kaitlyn M. Brown,** Assistant Professor, California State University, Northridge

"...is a 'must-have' for anthropology instructors and departments as they respond to changes in the discipline. It provides the foundation for redesigning traditional courses and reshaping curricula in an era in which students must have the understanding and skills of application and practice for non-academic careers."

— **Juliana McDonald,** Associate Professor, University of Kentucky

TABLE OF CONTENTS

PREFACE

If you are teaching anthropology and would like to learn about how to make your curriculum more career-oriented, then this book is for you.

Most anthropology students, as we all know, will not go on to become anthropology professors. Instead, they will *practice* anthropology in various ways, in whatever career they choose.

Some of them will have professional careers **in anthropology**, as practitioners, across a wide range of domains. Others – especially undergraduates – will have careers **with anthropology**, where they will find ways to use what they have learned, no matter what it is they are doing.

All of them will benefit from an academic curriculum which links anthropological knowledge and skills to how that knowledge and those skills are applied in everyday life.

And for those students intent upon an academic career, a better understanding of how their discipline is used outside the walls of the academy will build their capacity to teach anthropology to others. They will also become more adept at outreach, partnering with a wider group of stakeholders including private and nonprofit organizations as well as local, state and federal government agencies.

This book is but one of numerous resources that ACRN has developed to help instructors, students and practitioners. Please consider joining our network and taking part in what has become a robust and exciting professional conversation about where our discipline is going, the ways in which it can have sustained impact, and how we can all help to get it there.

ACKNOWLEDGEMENTS

Many individuals contributed to the development of *Teaching Tools for Anthropology Careers*. We began developing the first instructor tools in 2022, expanding them later to include tools useful for anthropology departments. We are grateful for the efforts of the following authors:

Elizabeth K. Briody

Keri Vacanti Brondo

Barry Dornfeld

Ken C. Erickson

Jonathan Geyer

Irene Greene

Carla Guerrón Montero

Sarah Heinemeier

Aimee E. Huard

Ed Liebow

Priscilla Rachun Linn

Edward (Ted) Maclin

Zahra Malik

Jeff Martin

Janelle-Marie Moreno

Robert McCallum

Riall W. Nolan

Megan O'Brien-Rene

Emma Pramuk

Laurie Schwede

Susan Squires

Kedron Thomas

Jennifer Trivedi

Andrew Walsh

Michael Wesch

Jiangjiang (JJ) Wu

Tools are assessed by multiple reviewers to ensure they are accurate and complete. Numerous people stepped up to play this role, for which we are very thankful:

Peter Benson

Elizabeth K. Briody

Sherrylyn H. Briller

Shan-Estelle Brown

Melissa Cefkin

Christopher Cosby

Barry Dornfeld

E. Paul Durrenberger

Emery R. Eaves

Jan English-Lueck

Suzan Erem

Lindsey R. Feldman

David M. Fetterman

Melissa Fisher

Adam Gamwell

Kristine McKenzie Gentry

Lise Byars George

Jonathan Geyer

Kathleen Gillogly

Kristin Hedges

Joyce Henderson

David Himmelgreen

Yuson Jung

Nicole C. Kellett

Charles Klein

Dawn Lehman

Jordan Levy

Ed Liebow

Martha Lincoln

Priscilla Rachun Linn

Edward (Ted) Maclin

Timothy de Waal Malefyt

Jeff Martin

Juliana McDonald

Robert J. Morais

Melissa Nelson

Elizabeth G. (Libby) Pfeffer

Sarah Renkert

Audrey Ricke

Marc S. Robinson

Jose L. Santos

Elizabeth (Beth) Schill

Sarah Schmidt

Tara Schwegler

Jamie E. Shenton

Jenessa Mae Spears

Phil Surles

Bryan Tilt

Jennifer Trivedi

Melissa Vogel

Sharon E. Watson

Michael Wesch

Laura Wangsness Willemsen

We also appreciate the time and interest of a number of anthropology professors to review some of the book's content and tools prior to publication. They offered short testimonials based on their familiarity with the materials and ACRN generally. The testimonials appear in the book and on the anthrocareerready.net website.

Kaitlyn M. Brown

Shan-Estelle Brown

Emily Brunson

Alejandro Cerón

A.J. Faas

Cynthia Grace-McCaskey

Anne L. Grauer

Kenneth Maes

Juliana McDonald

Mark Moritz

Melissa A. Nelson

Michael Wesch

Jonna Yarrington

Finally, we are grateful for the technical assistance we received from two ACRN interns in formatting the text, creating the graphics, and formatting the tools:

Tereza Emilova

Irene Greene

INTRODUCTION

CHANGING TIMES

Anthropology in the U.S. is facing numerous challenges. There has been a secular decline in student enrollments in our discipline, going back many years. More recently, anthropology has come under pressure from multiple quarters—students, parents, legislatures—to demonstrate relevance and career readiness

Currently, anthropology programs are facing a significant decline in enrollment across the U.S. There was a 23% decline in BA degrees between 2011-2023, while MA & PhD degrees dropped 12% and 19% (IPEDS, National Center for Education Statistics). As a result, many anthropology departments are being combined with other disciplines or shuttered.

Despite these negatives, we are also in the midst of several very positive trends. The growth of anthropological practice has continued, to the point where practitioners now constitute both the majority of anthropologists and, in many ways, the cutting edge of the discipline. Non-academic opportunities for graduates continue to grow, in stark contrast to the availability of academic jobs. No matter where you may be teaching anthropology, it is likely that most of your students will wind up in practice.

How well prepared are anthropology students for the workplace? The answer is, at almost every institution, "not as well as they could be."

Preparing anthropology graduates for the careers that await them provides an opportunity for the discipline to grow its professional side—not to replace what we already do, but to enhance and complement it. Anthropology excels at critique and analysis; to these skills, we need to add problem solving, if we expect anthropology to be relevant in today's world.

Graduates need skills and training in the application of their discipline, as well as the ability to work with others in fast-moving, demanding environments. This assertion is as true for our undergraduate majors as it is for our PhD candidates. To all of them—BA, MA, or PhD holders—we owe training which enables them to contribute positively to building a better world for us all.

THE ANTHROPOLOGY CAREER READINESS NETWORK

The Anthropology Career Readiness Network (ACRN) began in 2021. Since then, we have been working to help improve the teaching of anthropology so that students are prepared to meet the challenges and opportunities they will face in the workplace and beyond.

We are a group of volunteers composed of students, instructors, and practitioners working collaboratively. We are flexible and responsive, drawing on the skills and experiences of these groups. In our work, we encourage the co-thinking, co-creation and problem solving which are so characteristic of practice. We encourage our members to move beyond critique to solutions, and to make them accessible to as many people as possible, preferably without paywalls or other restrictions.

Our approach to career preparation with students is informed by the experience of practitioners. We share practitioner insights with instructors, helping them to learn how they can improve the career readiness of their students. Our operating model—translating the lessons of practice into relevant academic training—is designed to prepare the next generation of students and instructors for the opportunities and challenges of the future.

ACRN has engaged in research, focus groups and conversations with practitioners in the field to learn about what they needed to know to apply anthropology, and then to design mechanisms to bring solutions into the classroom. Our goal is not to challenge current anthropological training but rather to extend it, so that graduates are prepared for careers outside the academy.

Publications are one way we accomplish this goal. We also develop "tools"–resources which incorporate "how-to" information, insights and advice. For students and job seekers, tool topics relate to the "career journey" including skill development, methods, job search and interviewing, and problem solving. In addition, we have produced numerous tools tied to specific careers in which anthropologists work. For instructors, tool topics fall into two main groups: 1) strengthening understanding and management of the department's changing environment; and 2) integrating career readiness into the curriculum and departmental programming.

Another strategy for improving career readiness is through advising. ACRN works with anthropology programs to help them develop and implement their own career readiness plans. We also advise on client-based class projects in which a professor and students work to address an important problem identified by clients. In addition, we organize webinars, training workshops, consultations, discussions and presentations, here in the U.S. and abroad. We manage a website which is constantly being updated. We have a bi-monthly newsletter and a bi-monthly virtual meeting for our members.

STRENGTHENING THE CURRICULUM

The materials in this book are based on ACRN's career-ready curriculum model (Nolan & Briody 2023). A series of ACRN discussions with students and practitioners, as well as several in-depth research surveys of practitioners contributed to its creation. Figure 1 shows an updated version of the career ready curriculum.

Figure 1. The Career Ready Curriculum, aka Curriculum "Wheel"

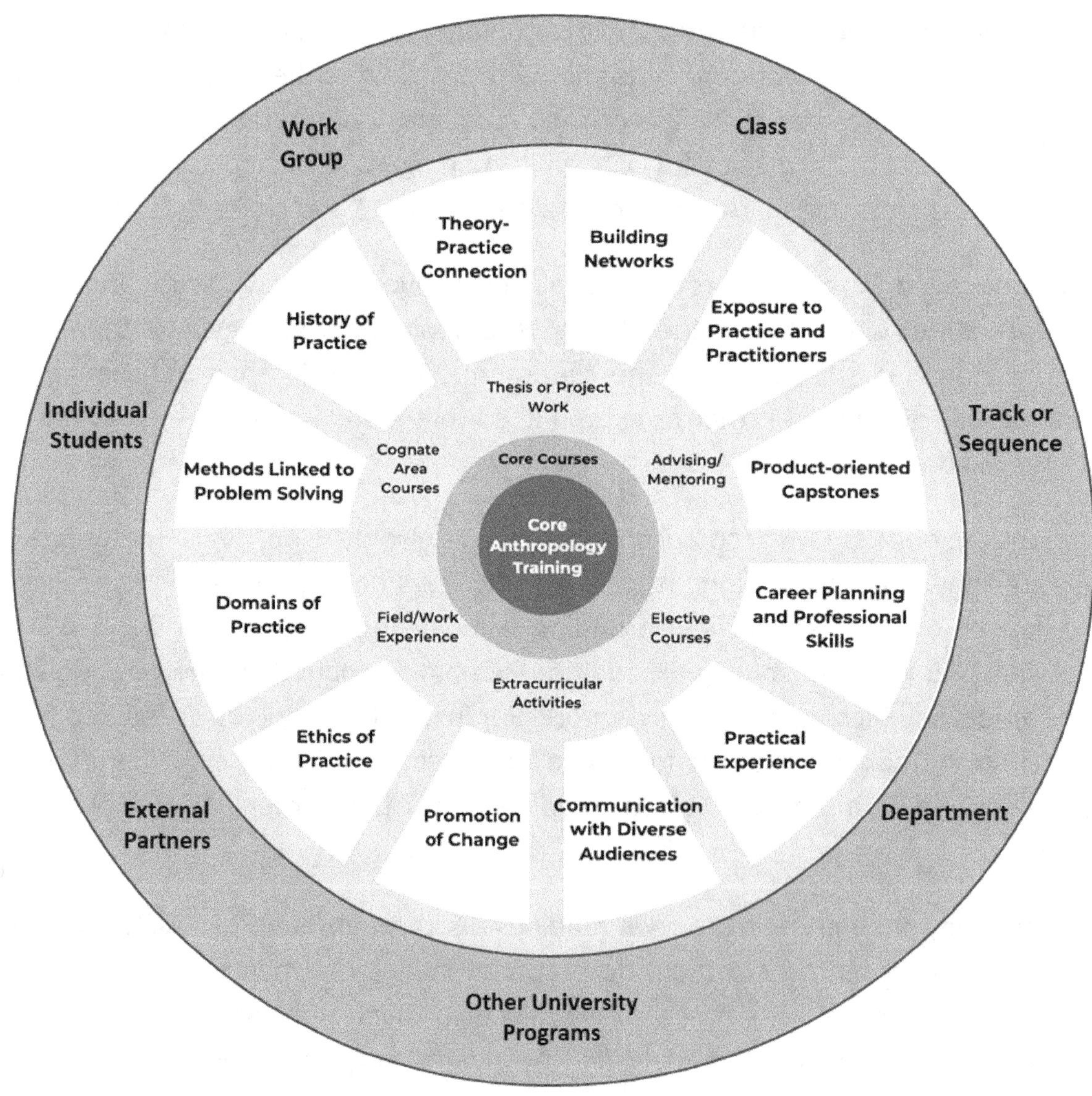

Change in academic programs happens in a variety of ways and at a variety of levels. This volume contains a range of outlines, templates, tools and suggestions for you to use, individually and as a department, as you build capacity in anthropology to adjust to the numerous pressures affecting higher education, now and in the future.

This curriculum "wheel" is a guide to embedding career readiness into a department's existing curriculum. The **hub** of the wheel reflects the traditional core anthropological training as offered by most existing programs. In addition to core training, departments usually offer other options for students which may include cognate courses, field experience, electives, advising, thesis or project work. Various extracurricular activities may also be available, such as language learning.

The **spokes** of the wheel represent extensions and enhancements of the traditional anthropology curriculum, designed to highlight career readiness. These elements are not replacements for the existing curriculum, but extensions of it. ACRN identified 12 of these basic areas or elements. A department may have some or none of these elements in place.

Finally, the **outer rim** of the wheel represents a recent modification to the model. It lists the various modalities through which students learn these elements, ranging from individualized learning through traditional classes, work groups, class projects, and work with outside partners or programs.

ESSENTIAL CONCEPTS FOR ANTHROPOLOGICAL PRACTICE

We highlight here four concepts worth interweaving into anthropology courses so that students get repeated exposure to and practice with them. None are specifically anthropological, but when combined with anthropological content, they can be powerful catalysts for raising awareness of anthropology's value. The tools mentioned below can be found on our website under Job Seeker and Career Tools or in *Career Tools for Anthropology: An Anthropology Career Readiness Workbook* (Studebaker et al, 2024). We continue to develop new tools; check the website regularly for new additions.

Communication is the first concept or skill. In anthropology, it often refers to writing, speaking, or visual media. Students get some practice with different forms of communication in writing papers or presenting their work in class. However, students lack experience in interacting with those who do not understand the field of anthropology (e.g., peers from other disciplines, family members, work supervisors) and how it can be useful in organizations and communities. We suggest a greater focus on practicing conversations and interviews so that students learn to respond clearly, concisely, and confidently. The following tools can be useful in teaching how to communicate about anthropology to different audiences, but especially prospective employers:

- Translating Anthropology Skills to the Workplace

- Explaining Anthropology to People in Your Life

- Crafting Engaging Stories

- Job Interview Strategies

- Interviewing with the STAR Method

- Public Speaking

Networking is a concept familiar to many who have searched for work. Anthropologists are familiar with it as well, particularly since they must activate their networking skills as they begin a field project in a new location. Yet, we have discovered in our workshops and webinars with students that they view networks negatively. They seem to consider networking a first cousin of nepotism, and therefore distasteful and providing an unfair advantage. We suggest instructors advocate and teach networking basics, coordinate alumni events where students engage in networking, and require students to build and expand their professional network by documenting their contacts. ACRN has both tools and webinars for students to assist you including:

- Networking and Informational Interviews

- Mastering the Elevator Pitch

- Expanding Your Professional Network into a New Area of Work

- Exploring Domains of Practice

- Setting Up and Conducting Informational Interviews

The third concept is **collaboration**. So much of anthropological training has been based on the model of the individual learner and "lone wolf" researcher. Instructors would do well to shift to a collaborative focus on projects, events, and other learning activities because hiring managers look for collaborative experience in job candidates. Client-based class projects are one obvious mechanism for getting students to work together on data collection, analysis, and delivery of results and recommendations to the client. Even shorter-term exercises such as sending pairs of students to conduct an informational interview with a practitioner—also a form of networking—can make such tasks easier and more enjoyable. Various resources related to collaboration are covered later in the book.

The last concept, **problem solving**, is one that academic anthropologists should be able to appreciate because they are continually dealing with research issues, among other problems. However, practitioners take problem solving to the next level. Not only do they address challenges in conducting research, but they also are focused on developing and testing solutions that can address the problem being researched directly. Employers seek job candidates who have a solutions-oriented mindset, a "can-do" spirit, and the expertise to gather insights, analyze alternatives, troubleshoot, and propose recommendations. By learning to treat the job search as fieldwork, these tools can introduce students to that problem-solving focus:

- <u>What Can You Do with a Degree in Anthropology?</u>

- <u>Showcasing Anthropology to Employers</u>

- <u>Client Engagement Best Practices</u>

This book presents a broad set of instructor tools which relate directly or indirectly to the curriculum wheel. We introduce most of these tools in the first two chapters of the book: **Moving Your Department Ahead**; and **Building Career Readiness into Your Courses**. We then follow with a third chapter entitled **Securing Anthropology's Future**. Taken together, these three chapters offer suggestions for building capacity within departments for career-ready training, and ultimately, for strengthening the discipline at a time of change and challenge.

CHAPTER 1: MOVING YOUR DEPARTMENT AHEAD

Now we turn to your department. This chapter presents a selection of tools which will help you plan for the future. Some of these approaches are probably well-known to members of your department in that they are specifically anthropological. Others relate to overall organizational change and development.

Departments seek "change" for different reasons. Some are interested in beginning new programs or going in new directions, while others seek to add to or improve existing offerings. Dominating the higher education landscape are various external pressures to make changes. Stakeholders such as state legislatures and the federal government are demanding a higher return on investment for a university education—so much so that "ROI" is routinely encountered in department discussions. Parents and students increasingly seek greater assurance that an anthropology major will lead to job prospects post-graduation. Career readiness is the key strategy to address such pressures.

Whatever the impetus for change, the process requires group coordination, discussion, and strategic decision making within your department. The tools in this section do not provide solutions but rather describe processes of various kinds that you can draw on as you chart your course.

UNDERSTANDING THE BIG PICTURE

For over four decades, increasing numbers of practitioners have been actively engaged in transforming anthropology. Not only have they published and presented their work in industry, nonprofits, and government to anthropological audiences (e.g., annual meetings, journal publications), but they have tackled many different organizational and community problems and implemented solutions. Their careers represent countless new versions of anthropological field work. These practitioners are important sources of both expertise and experience for anthropology's new career directions.

The National Association for the Practice of Anthropology (NAPA), established in 1983 as a section of the American Anthropological Association (AAA), spearheaded documentation of practitioner careers. First, it created the *NAPA Bulletins* which published numerous accounts of the roles in which anthropologists worked (Davis et al. 1987; Guerrón Montero 2008;

Hanson et al. 1988; Meerwarth et al. 2008; Reed 1997; Sabloff 2000; Wasson 2006); the *NAPA Bulletins* subsequently evolved into the journal *Annals of Anthropological Practice*. Second, NAPA sponsored and produced the first careers video in 1994, *Anthropologists at Work: Careers Making a Difference* (Briody and Bodo 1994; Briody 1995). Two other careers videos were produced—*Applying Anthropology: Careers that Count* (2005) and *Beyond Ethnography: Corporate and Design Anthropology* (2008)—and subsequently disseminated by the AAA. Third, it published two reports on the careers of MA-degree holders (Fiske et al. 2010; Hawvermale et al. 2020). Since 2022, NAPA has featured the careers of anthropologists in short conversational videos in its sNAPAshots' series (https://practicinganthropology.org/blog/snapashots-conversations-with-professional-practicing-and-applied-anthropologists/, accessed December 20, 2025).

Other anthropologists have also written about careers held by anthropologists outside the academy—both in the U.S. and abroad. The form in which these career insights are presented range from vignettes to full-length chapters (Artz and Koycheva 2025; Nolan 2013; Nolan 2026; Oliveira 2013; Podjed and Guerrón Montero 2026; Strang 2021; Trester 2022) to video (Altimare 2008; Gamwell et al. 20022; Smiley 2005). The careers of some practitioners are also documented in the Society for Applied Anthropology's Oral History Project (https://appliedanthro.org/resources-projects/oral-history-project/, accessed January 12, 2026).

Identifying Missing Elements from Anthropology Training

How many times have we heard the statement that anthropology is so versatile that graduates can find work in virtually any organizational setting? While many might agree with that adage, *how* a person prepares for a future career, engages in the job search, and secures employment are not typically taught in bachelor or graduate programs. Consequently, anthropology graduates have had to "reinvent the wheel" repeatedly to figure out how to approach the job market and persuade hiring managers to bring them on board. The one formalized source of support for job seekers was NAPA's Mentor Program, established in 1990. It has paired hundreds of mentors with mentees, offering them career guidance with networking and resume assistance.

ACRN's approach was different. When we launched ACRN in 2021, we directed our attention primarily to the preparation and skills anthropologists would need in their careers, rather than the careers themselves. We soon formed several working groups on key topics related to anthropological training and career readiness. These groups assessed the current state of the training and identified areas of success as well as improvement by involving practitioners and applied anthropology instructors in the effort. Their work resulted in the development of some initial instructor tools in 2022. These tools, expanded and improved, laid the groundwork for two career readiness "checklist" tools, described later in this book.

We then expanded our understanding of the applicability and usefulness of anthropological training in the U.S. by surveying practitioners working in industry, nonprofits, and government. Because this study turned out to be highly informative and useful for ACRN, we take some time here to describe it in detail.

ACRN's Delphi Survey

Two rounds of a Delphi survey of current practitioners were conducted to understand the gaps in anthropological training relating to career exploration and search, career entry, and job performance overall (Nolan and Briody 2024). In Round 1, practitioners were asked to respond to the following prompts:

> *1) In terms of equipping you to find your job in practice, what specific things would have been helpful for you to have learned as part of your academic program? Please write down up to 10 specific things, using one- or two-word descriptors.*

> *2) In terms of being able to do your job in a successful and satisfactory manner, what specific things would have been helpful for you to have learned as part of your academic program? Please write down up to 10 specific things, using one- or two-word descriptors.*

We received 227 responses to Question 1, and 237 responses to Question 2. The responses were analyzed separately.

When it comes to the question of finding or getting a job, Networking and Connections and Job Search Strategy and Skills were the clear priorities followed by Translating Anthropology to Industry (See Figure 2).

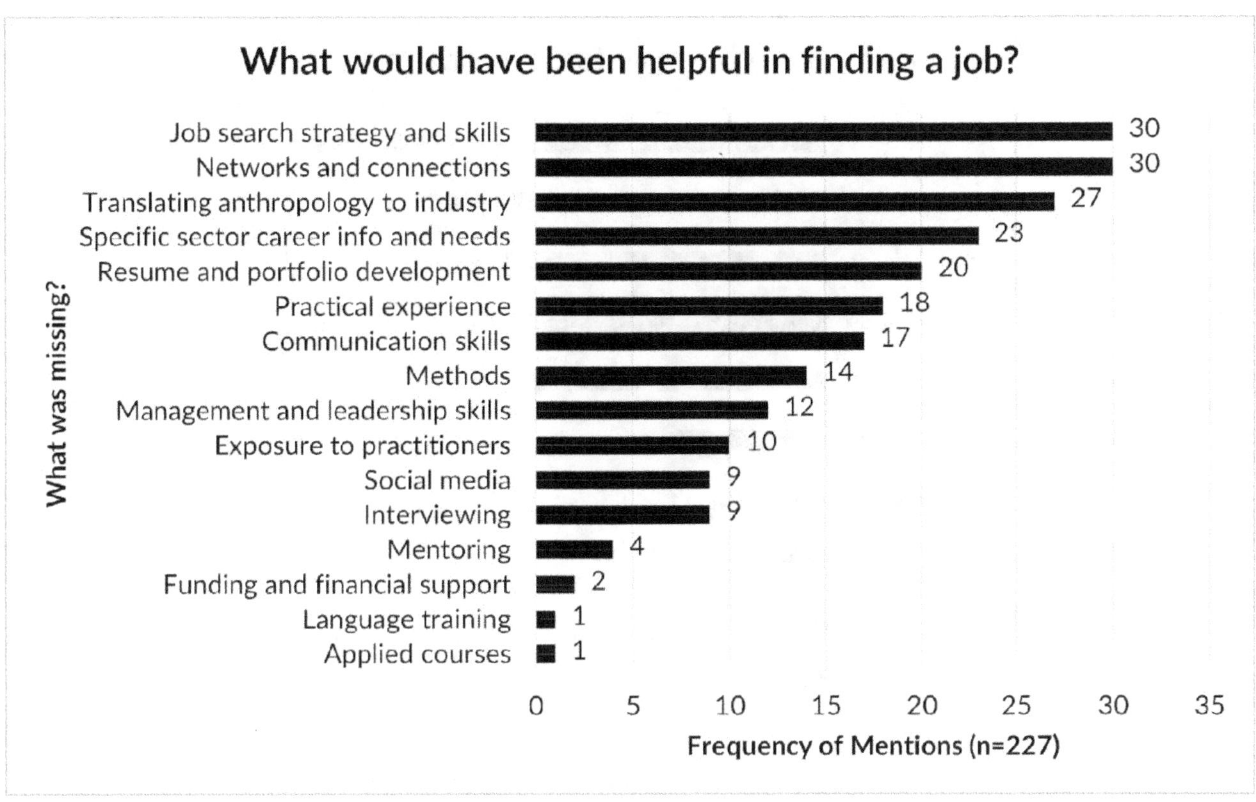

Practitioners also wanted guidance on how to build professional networks. Network connections can open doors to new career opportunities, and in tight job markets, networking may be the difference between securing a job and not landing one. To do an informed job search, practitioners wanted to know more about job hunting specifically for careers in business, nonprofits, and/or government; they also wanted a better understanding of the differences across these sectors. Consequently, they needed assistance on how to translate their anthropological skills and experience to make the case for getting hired to potential employers.

When it comes to doing their job, methods predominated, followed by communication and project planning and management skills (See Figure 3).

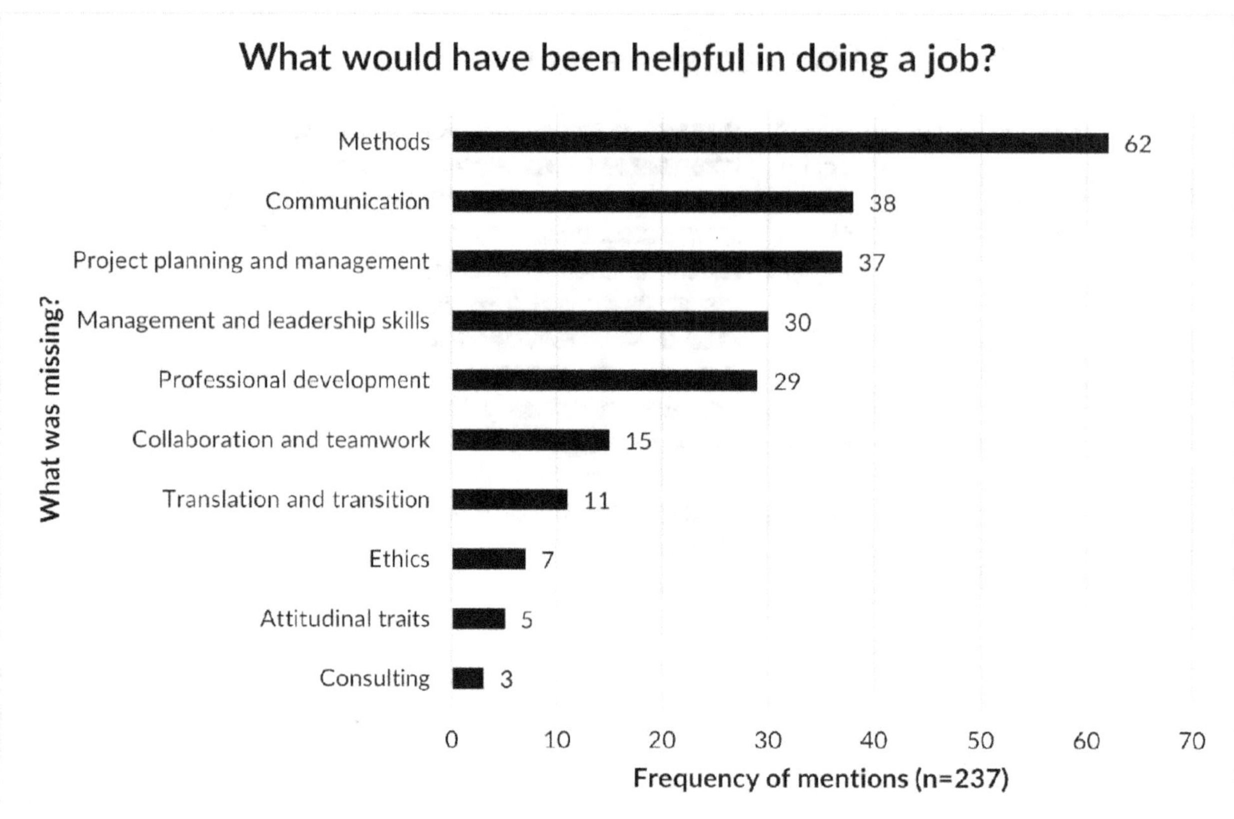

Practitioners report regularly that they are valued most for their methods (i.e., their ability to find things out). Practitioners usually present their findings to those without an anthropology background; understanding how to communicate to diverse audiences is often a job requirement. Much of what practitioners do at work is project-based, requiring both skills in project planning and management.

Round 2 of the Delphi survey dug deeper into the question of methods, and practitioners were asked to reply to the following prompt:

> *In Round One, many of you indicated a need for more training in methods, particularly those methods not (yet) part of the "traditional" ethnographic research portfolio. Below, we'd like you to list up to ten different methods that you use or have used in your work, which were not necessarily part of your academic training. You can be as specific as you want here. Use key words or short phrases where possible.*

We received a total of 159 responses from 34 people. The responses fell into three distinctive categories (See Figure 4).

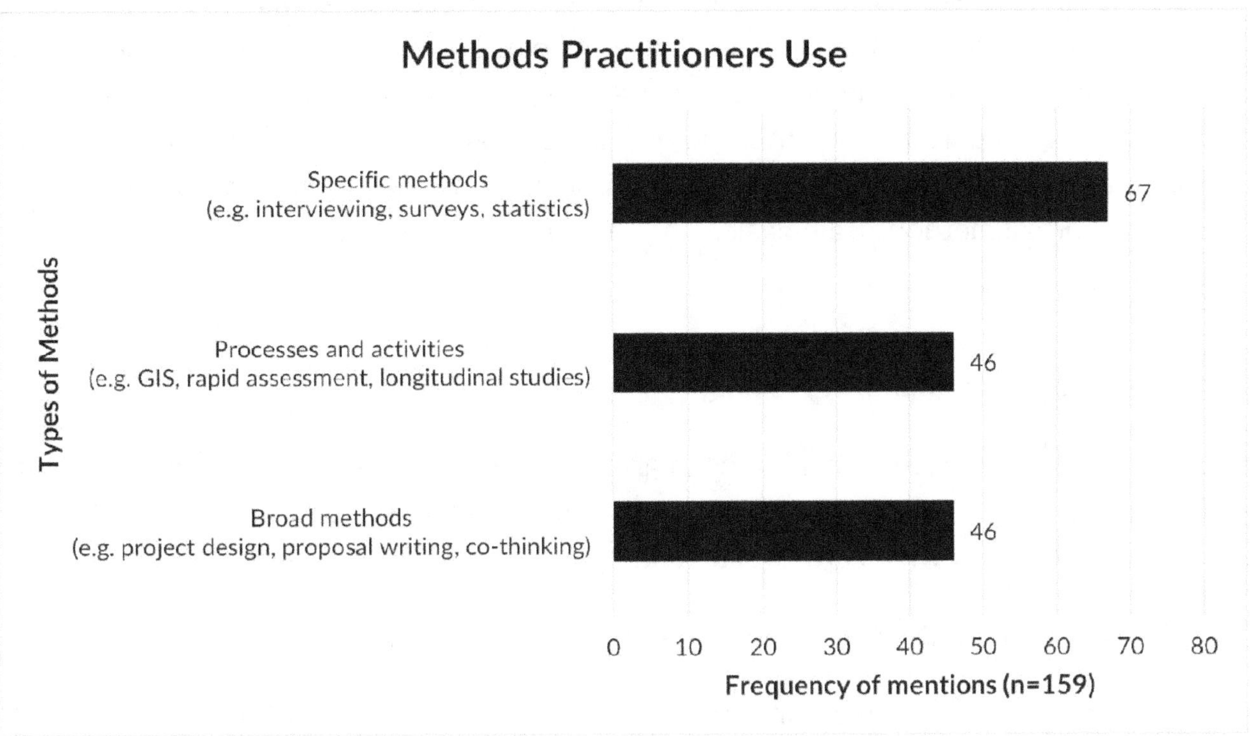

Specific methods (N=67) included techniques that most traditionally trained anthropologists would be aware of (e.g., interviewing, statistics, survey work). Delphi respondents suggested several newer techniques, such as sketching and wireframing, digital ethnography, and video analysis.

Broad Methods are general methods (N=46) including techniques which could be done (and are done) in different ways. Rapid assessment was a typical example here. Longitudinal studies, usability studies, Geographic Information System (GIS), and web-scraping were others.

Processes and Activities represent a third category (N=46). While this category may include a component of data collection, it is really focused on something different: "getting things done." Most of the responses concerned project design and management, workshops, co-thinking and co-creation, and crafting pitches or proposals to clients.

From this analysis, two categories of methods emerged: methods designed to find things out and methods designed to get things done. Processes and activities may not be considered "methods" in most anthropology programs, but these results show how leading change and change management are important parts of most practitioner jobs.

Given the wide range of different methods and their rapid evolution in the workplace—AI technology being a great example—departments would be best served by covering the basic anthropology methods, and then teaching students how to evaluate, choose, and learn new methods themselves. Knowing how to select and deploy methods are essential skills once on the job. It is important for anthropology departments to ensure that the basics of anthropology methods are offered and required, since some practitioners report graduating without any formal methods training, leaving them to find their way on their own.

Addressing Missing Elements in Training

ACRN's approach to this issue continues to grow and expand as we listen to and work with departments and practitioners. Based on these early results, we focused on the following calls to action, many of which are directly addressed throughout this book:

- Add more methods courses (e.g., content analysis, mixed methods).

- Build connections with organizations (e.g., create pipelines for internships and jobs).

- Design skills-based fieldwork.

- Develop class projects with external clients to learn how to diagnose and address problems.

- Explore and utilize available career resources to help guide career planning.

- Invite practitioners to your courses or department (e.g., to serve on a career panel, network with students, deliver a workshop).

- Offer professional development training in conjunction with available campus resources (e.g., Career Services).

- Seek program alumni mentoring for students and advising for departments.

Adopting Components of Successful Applied Programs

Earlier research (Briody & Nolan 2013) on characteristics of applied programs identified some key components of the best of them. Departments today desiring to become more career oriented might consider how to develop or encourage these characteristics in their own offerings.

What made an applied department particularly successful? Here were some of the more salient findings:

- These departments tended to be more integrated and collaborative, with consensus among faculty as to the overall content of the curriculum.

- They offered more in the way of applied courses and experiences, more opportunity for collaborative work among students, and more engagement with outside organizations.

- They recognized that not all their graduates would seek academic positions.

- Instead of individual fieldwork, they emphasized internships and class projects.

- In addition to teaching theory and method, they integrated those domains with group-based problem-solving experiences.

- In addition to contact with individual professors, they facilitated contacts with alumni and practitioners.

While every department is unique, and every program will develop career readiness in its own way, several key points seem to be emerging:

- There needs to be broad agreement on the value and purpose of career-ready initiatives across the department.

- Career-ready activities need to be broadly infused within the curriculum, and not relegated to one or two courses or activities.

- Theory, method and critical thinking need to be linked to a concern for problem identification and problem solving.

- Students should be exposed as early as possible to a variety of career possibilities, through contact with actual individuals if possible.

- Students should be given the opportunity to develop experience with, and skills in, collaboration and groupwork.

In our work with departments, ACRN found a range of activities employed to bring career readiness into the program (Ramer et al 2022). Some of these activities are arranged, along a continuum of increasing effort and complexity (See Figure 5). The simplest is the introduction of an in-class activity focused on an applied topic. This can be followed by an entire course dealing with the application of anthropology to various domains. As more activities, courses, certificates and/or degrees are added, the level of effort climbs appreciably.

Figure 5. Career Readiness Activities by Level of Effort and Complexity

One or more applied classes	Capstone courses	Involvement with alumni	Majors or minors	Organizational & community-based projects
In-class activities	A suite of classes	Courses with other disciplines	Certificate programs	Internships or practicums

Increasing level of effort and complexity

Barriers to success included the research and publishing demands of a tenure-track role, limited numbers of instructors, and other constraints on time and resources. However, those that saw success focused on building robust internal and external networks. They also created plans for sustainability beyond the existing instructors by embedding their changes into the department and its policies.

While requiring creativity and resilience, departments can be successful when many or all the following components are introduced and maintained:

- Applied courses are taught by several instructors, not a "champion" professor.

- Integration of problem solving is interwoven throughout the curriculum in courses associated with theory, methods, and field/lab/work experiences.

- Introduction to anthropology careers happens early in the program (e.g., ANTH 101).

- Networking with alumni, practitioners, and outside organizations occurs routinely.

- Practitioner involvement takes many forms: in mentoring students, offering guest lectures, workshops, and Q&A career sessions, advising on capacity building, and providing internships.

- Client-based projects are led by instructors in organizations and community settings.

- Students enroll in a career-oriented professionalism course early in the program.

- Professors expose students to interdisciplinary work through courses and projects.

- Internships take place in business, government and non-profit organizations.

- Experiential and product-oriented capstone projects (e.g., portfolios, presentations, reports, models) synthesize career readiness lessons.

- A convergence of interests by organizational/community partners and instructors helps build and sustain the program.

- Anthropology program efforts are endorsed by Institutional administration.

- A degree or certificate identifies program emphases (e.g., "applied medical anthropology") when appropriate.

Addressing Challenges Posed by Applied Programs

Through our research, we also learned that applied programs generally faced challenges—whether internally to the department, in relation to the wider university, or relative to anthropology programs across universities:

- Applied anthropology is a minor emphasis in most programs.

- There is little, if any, cohesion in how applied anthropology is taught.

- Practitioners themselves are conspicuously absent from most programs.

- There is little policy support for applied anthropology in many institutions.

- Methods, if taught, are often unrelated to problem solving and change making.

- There are few mechanisms for promoting the sustainability of changes which are implemented.

Building career readiness into your program is an ongoing activity, and it will not be done by simply introducing a few new courses or renaming others. There will be continued discussion within the discipline about the meaning and value of applied and practicing anthropology, and there will sometimes be differences and disagreements that emerge and must be addressed.

It is important to ensure that such discussions do not derail the work that you are doing together. With that in mind, here are a few suggestions for managing disagreement and conflict, should they arise:

- Try to identify common interests and aspirations and build on them.

- Dig underneath stated positions to uncover the interests and concerns which underlie them.

- Separate problems from people—do not make your disagreements personal.

- Celebrate success and acknowledge effort.

- Seek objective criteria and measures whenever possible for what you are attempting—indicators that everyone can agree on.

- Break large and complex issues and problems into their smaller components and tackle them one by one.

- Finally, recognize that many departments face similar problems. Find out how others have addressed their issues. Ask whether their solutions might work for your program.

Anthropology departments can be changemakers. The tools in this book (presented in numbered order at the end) will provide you with the skills and resources to take on the challenges of introducing and sustaining change. To get you launched on your own career readiness voyage, we suggest you begin with this tool: "Your Career Ready Department Checklist." It will help you evaluate where career readiness stands in your department, identify some of your departmental goals and objectives, and help you imagine where your department might head in the future. As you read through the tool, you will see that department efforts are designed to promote career readiness. Features of this tool emphasize both engagement with external partners (e.g., alumni, internship supervisors) and the coordination of department-wide activities to benefit students.

<u>1. Your Career Ready Department Checklist</u>

Planning Change

Once you have decided that changes in your anthropology program are warranted, you will need to engage in discussions, decisions, and planning. You begin this process with your department colleagues, extending it later to include other stakeholders within and beyond your campus.

Getting Started with the Departmental Advisory Initiative

In this section, we introduce tools we incorporate in our engagements with universities participating in the Departmental Advisory Initiative (DAI). An overview of the program and how it works is presented in "The Departmental Advisory Initiative" tool. DAI facilitators guide, coach, and advise anthropology programs in crafting and then implementing their own career readiness implementation plan. DAI typically lasts just over one year, with quarterly "check-ins" from facilitators following a campus visit.

2. The Departmental Advisory Initiative

The next five tools are used during the DAI campus visit. Facilitators share a compilation of departmental responses to a SWOT analysis. SWOT, an acronym standing for Strengths, Weaknesses, Opportunities, and Threats, reveals perspectives on departmental assets as well as challenges—whether internal or external. "Using SWOT to Prepare for Change" suggests analyses that enable department members to understand the possibilities open to them given their current circumstances.

3. Using SWOT to Prepare for Change

The SWOT analysis works hand in hand with the ecosystem analysis. Careful focus on your ecosystem will allow your department to ascertain the potential for new networks, information, and sources of support. "Exploring Your Ecosystem to Expand Connections" provides a framework when investigating the environment in which you are situated.

4. Exploring Your Ecosystem to Expand Connections

Some people in, or connected to, your ecosystem have influence over the plans you develop and the decisions you make. We discuss stakeholders (e.g., administrators, local organizational leaders, donors) in relation to your goals. The "Analyzing Stakeholders to Build Support" tool goes beyond identifying your stakeholders. It helps you think through why and how those stakeholders might be persuaded of your initiative's value, what they might gain, and you might connect with them.

5. Analyzing Stakeholders to Build Support

We often finish by inviting the department to complete a "concept map" to clarify what they mean by the concept career readiness. We have found that this exercise from the tool "Finding Clarity with Concept Maps" helps build consensus on the term, as well as indicating some important areas for future activity.

6. Finding Clarity with Concept Maps

Once the concept map exercise on career readiness has been completed, it should be a relatively simple step to the next tool used during a DAI campus visit: "Establishing Common Ground on Career Readiness." This tool helps anthropology departments identify and reach agreement on a shared view of their program's purpose and direction.

7. Establishing Common Ground on Career Readiness

The final tool in this section is called "Drafting Your Anthropology Roadmap." This tool emerged as a tangible product from our DAI visit to the University of Delaware; it has since been discussed with all subsequent universities who have participated in DAI. The roadmap is a visual portrayal of the key areas of knowledge, skills, and experiences that students gain in their anthropology program.

8. Drafting Your Anthropology Department Roadmap

The roadmap depicted in Figure 6 illustrates the anthropology major at the University of Delaware, an undergraduate-only program. To create it, professors identified the content students learned in each of their courses, the skills they acquired and practiced, and work-related and professional activities which would help familiarize them with career options. Once this information was compiled and analyzed, the department had drafted, and eventually finalized, their roadmap.

Figure 6. The Roadmap for the Anthropology Major at the University of Delaware

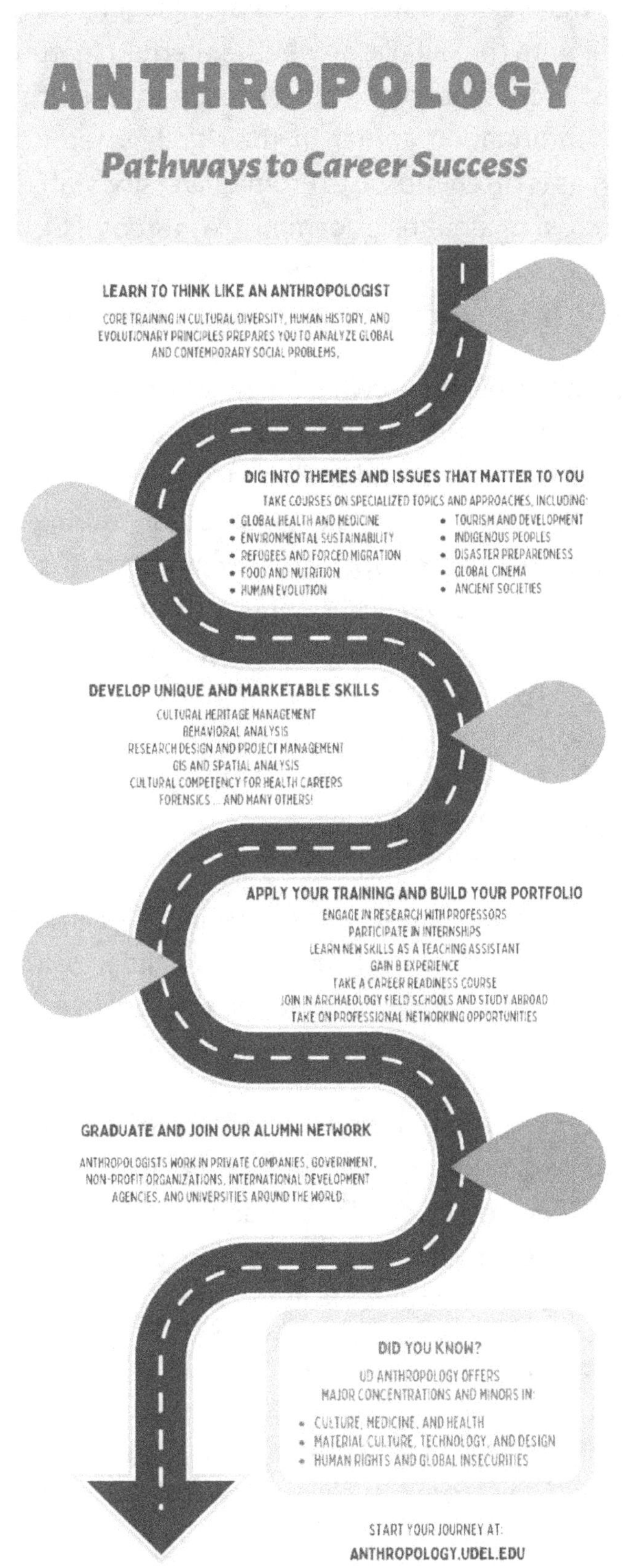

In numerous discussions, instructors learned from each other, their students, and university staff. While instructors may have known that their colleagues taught specific courses, they were typically unfamiliar with the details, or whether certain features overlapped with those taught in other courses. From students, instructors discovered that their students needed internships and career information earlier in their college education rather than on the threshold of graduation as is often the case. From university staff, instructors learned about the availability of unknown or unfamiliar campus resources—such as the Student Success Center and Career Services Center. All this dialogue revealed new opportunities for students which subsequently have become integral to Delaware's anthropology program.

Response to the roadmap has been overwhelmingly positive. Administrators who have seen it have offered rave reviews for its compilation, creativity, and visual appeal. Current students reference it both to understand their near-term future in relation to the past and to plan out their upcoming course schedules. Repeatedly during "Blue and Golden Days," anthropology's booth has been packed with prospective students and their parents eager to get a closer look at the massive vertical banner. It was not long after the department roadmap was finalized that roadmaps for the anthropology minors and concentrations were designed, produced, and displayed.

Generating Ideas and Making Decisions

Anthropology departments that do not participate in DAI can still take advantage of the tools associated with it. We recommend setting aside time to work with your colleagues, asking someone to serve as facilitator. In addition to the tools previously discussed, we offer another set related to idea generation and decision making.

The tool, "Putting Force Field Analysis to Work," is helpful as you contemplate a specific change. The driving and resisting forces for the change you seek are listed and analyzed in relation to each other. Reducing or eliminating some of the resisting forces is typically a successful strategy, followed by strengthening one or more of the driving forces or identifying a new driving force that can be added.

9. Putting Force Field Analysis to Work

You may want to hold a brainstorming session with members of your department on any number of issues. "Using Brainstorming for Collaborative Problem Solving" is a tool that offers tips for generating new ideas as well as building on the ideas of others. It is especially beneficial when you are starting something new.

10. Using Brainstorming for Collaborative Problem Solving

We include two tools for making decisions. Some decisions have to be made by groups—such as you and your department colleagues. Consequently, the tool "Making Group Decisions through Discussion" offers suggestions for effective group meetings leading to decisions.

11. Making Group Decisions through Discussion

Another tool, "Moving Forward with Consensus Decision Making," offers a strategy for a collective decision-making process. The process is a collective one and implies a degree of compromise between what is preferred ideally and what is acceptable pragmatically.

12. Moving Forward with Consensus Decision Making

The final tool in this section is neither abstract, nor process oriented. Instead, it is a tool based on input—not by professors—but by students and recent graduates: "Improving Anthropology's Visibility on Campus." Compiled from focus group data, it identifies eight initiatives that departments can take to raise anthropology's profile and appeal to non-majors and the broader campus community. This tool complements "Boosting Anthropology Enrollments" (discussed in the next section) but offers distinctive perspectives and experiences that have not been previously captured. Current students, including members of anthropology clubs, may be interested in getting some of these initiatives off the ground!

13. Improving Anthropology's Visibility on Campus

Selling Change

Once you have decided on changes, you may still have to convince others that you are on the right path. Here are some tools you can use to promote your department and its activities, create allies and partners, and respond to objections from those who do not regard career readiness highly.

One of the most important partnerships a department can create is with its alumni. "Building Department-Alumni Connections" is a tool denoting the value alumni can offer their alma mater. Graduates are often eager to "give back" to the program that preceded their launch into the workplace. Interacting with current students in an informational interview, a workshop demonstrating methods and approaches used in their current job, or a Q&A session about their career enables an alum to share lessons and advice with the next generation. When strong relationships exist between a department and its alumni, other possibilities may include more extensive professional preparation (e.g., internships, mentoring).

14. Building Department-Alumni Connections

Alumni, as well as practitioners and/or organizational leaders, can serve as helpful advisors to your department. The tool "Launching and Sustaining a Community Advisory Board" presents an option for a longer-term commitment of willing and experienced professionals to your department. All parties have the potential to benefit from this relationship. The department typically seeks to learn about emerging workplace issues and bring in new ideas, networks, and resources. Advisory Board members appreciate building or enhancing their university connections, welcome their access to student interns/new hires and faculty expertise, and delight in making a difference in the lives of upcoming professionals.

15. Launching and Sustaining a Community Advisory Board

The issue of anthropology enrollments inevitably arises during our consultations with anthropology departments. As student numbers decline, anthropology is finding itself at a crossroads. In the tool "Boosting Anthropology Enrollments," ACRN emphasizes three long-term strategies: Curriculum changes (i.e., course updates, new course offerings), cultivating relationships both on and off campus—helpful in student career development, and marketing and public outreach about anthropology's value and relevance within and beyond academia. It is time for anthropology to become "sticky," that is, engaged and interwoven in the teaching and learning that occur across disciplines and with the general public.

16. Boosting Anthropology Enrollments

Finally, we want to acknowledge that "selling" change—even within your own department—can take time. Not all anthropologists accept the concept of career readiness, and even if they are open to it in theory, they may be unwilling to participate fully in preparing students for careers outside academia. ACRN developed a tool that you can share with your colleagues called "Addressing Instructor Concerns about Career Readiness." This tool presents numerous "objections" we have heard about career readiness and then offers an alternative perspective on each one. The tool also provides numerous strategies and tips to assist those who have expressed uncertainty or disinterest. A key theme underlying this tool is that helping students benefits the discipline of anthropology directly.

<u>17. Addressing Instructor Concerns about Career Readiness</u>

CHAPTER 2: BUILDING CAREER READINESS INTO YOUR COURSES

While the previous chapter focused on your department, this chapter provides tools for individual instructors to use in their courses. All these tools are designed to be used within an existing program to ensure anthropology students are career ready. These tools put the focus on how to use anthropological knowledge and approaches in problem solving.

LOOKING AT THE BIG PICTURE

There are many ways to introduce career-ready material and perspectives into teaching. These three tools will give you some useful ideas about where to start and how to focus your efforts.

The framework provided in the tool "A Career Ready Curriculum," presented in the Introduction, helps you conceptualize how anthropological practice can be integrated into your courses. As mentioned, the hub of the model illustrates the common or shared features of anthropology programs. The 12 elements alongside the spokes represent options for extending the content you present in class, activities for demonstrating student proficiency, and experiential learning that students acquire which will be valuable in their future work roles. All 12 elements help you to extend your curriculum so that anthropological practice is merged into it.

18. A Career Ready Curriculum

For the next tool, "A Training Matrix for Student Career Success," we expanded the hub and spoke model to contain a rim identifying key learning modalities (e.g., by oneself, in a work group, as part of a class). This tool serves as a template or heuristic device for examining learning modalities in relation to the elements found between the spokes. It can be used to plan where and how career-ready elements might be incorporated into an existing curriculum or individual course.

19. A Training Matrix for Student Career Success

"Your Career Ready Coursework Checklist" summarizes the many ways you can help students apply their knowledge and skills to a client or community problem, an imagined work environment, or their own job search. The suggestions enable students to practice networking, communicating, collaborating, and problem solving in and beyond the classroom. In addition, students benefit from interacting with and learning from role models, including alumni, practitioners, and community and organizational leaders.

20. Your Career Ready Coursework Checklist

RE-FOCUSING COURSE OFFERINGS

This section presents tools for specific topics. Some of these tools are stand alone, in the sense that they can be used by themselves. Others are designed to be used within existing courses, as extensions or additions to the syllabus.

Given how few students are exposed to anthropology until they arrive at college, it is essential to make a strong, positive impression in the first courses they take. ACRN has developed two tools that demonstrate the connections between the classroom and the workplace. "A Better ANTH 101" engages students directly in projects, experiential challenges, discussions of current issues, and career options. It includes insights into what anthropologists do in their work roles.

21. A Better ANTH 101

"A First Year Course in How Anthropology is Used in the World" concentrates student attention on specific domains of work (e.g., medical, business, AI/cyberculture). It deepens student awareness and knowledge of possible careers using anthropology and then tackles some of the challenges anthropologists face and the impact they have. In both courses, students can put themselves in the shoes of anthropologists to gauge their own interest in studying anthropology.

22. A First Year Course in How Anthropology is Used in the World

A tool that can heighten student interest in particular courses is called "Promoting Courses with a Dash of Pop Culture." Its intention is to persuade you of the value of catchy course titles and engaging content to attract those who otherwise might not register for your class. Incorporating pop culture as part of the course content might have even broader appeal.

The more students enrolling in anthropology courses, the greater the discipline's exposure and likely impact on them.

23. Promoting Courses with a Dash of Pop Culture

The tool "Bringing Anthropological Practice into the Classroom" emphasizes the value of educating students about anthropological work in the public, private, and nonprofit sectors. It offers a rationale for incorporating aspects of this work (e.g., readings, skill development, lectures) into *every* anthropology course rather than restricting it to specific courses such as applied anthropology, anthropological methods, and the capstone. To convey anthropological insights, the tool suggests several options for your students (e.g., short posts, videos, op-eds) that are better suited to public promotion of anthropology than say a term paper or final exam. Finally, the tool provides you with resources for finding practitioner case studies as well as speakers for your courses.

24. Bringing Anthropological Practice into the Classroom

Instructors have voiced their concerns to ACRN about the workload associated with career readiness. While updating any course requires some level of effort, we suggest that students can play a far greater role in coursework planning than they do at present. "Informational Interviewing in the Classroom" is a tool involving students directly in the preparation and management of a practitioner visit to a classroom to learn about that anthropologist's career. Your students not only decide who to invite, but they also organize the logistics of the visit, practice the informational interview technique, conduct the interview, debrief and document what they learned, and send a formal "thank you" to the anthropologist. Students benefit from the content provided by the practitioner, the process of preparing and carrying out an event, and the peer collaboration needed to bring the event off successfully. All these skills are transferable to future informational interviews and invitational events.

25. Informational Interviewing in the Classroom

The next two tools can be assigned as long-term projects or replace a midterm exam. "Teaching with Blogposts" is an ideal way for your students to learn to write an engaging piece in a succinct way without jargon. Writing a blogpost will also help your students develop and support their argument or point of view. This form of communication is easily transferrable to writing workplace memos, newsletters and reports that will be understood and appreciated by a diverse set of organizational stakeholders.

Get your students started by submitting a blogpost for ACRN's World of Work Blog: https://anthrocareerready.net/updates/world-of-work-blog/.

26. Teaching with Blogposts

A more challenging writing assignment involves learning to write an op-ed article. The "Teaching with Op-Eds" tool will help you to assist your students in developing a well-formulated argument about an issue, incorporating a story that engages readers, and proposing an actionable solution. This form of written communication teaches students to move beyond critique to resolve a current problem in society, a community, or organization. In doing so, you are teaching your students about policy development. Additionally, the AAA has offered "Write to Change the World" virtual workshops organized and facilitated by The Op-Ed Project (https://americananthro.org/news-advocacy/oped-project/, accessed January 17, 2026); these workshops can be valuable in helping anthropologists have greater impact in the world.

27. Teaching with Op-Eds

We are including one methodological tool in this book that is not well known among anthropologists: "Exploring Complex Issues with the Delphi Technique." You can use it in your own research or teach it your students. Delphi is a qualitative technique employing a purposive sample to investigate a topic about which little is known. It is easy to administer, rapid, and thorough, and is often a predecessor of in-depth data gathering.

28. Exploring Complex Issues with the Delphi Technique

The final tool in this section pertains to individualized or self-directed learning. We call this tool "Creating Learning Contracts for Student Growth." Learning contracts are a form of independent study but more flexible and under the control of the student. The tool helps you set up a learning contract and helps your students develop their skills as independent learners.

29. Creating Learning Contracts for Student Growth

This next set of tools will assist you in connecting your courses to outside networks and organizations. Think of them as a bridge between you and your students with workplaces in the public, private, and nonprofit sectors. These tools will enhance and extend student learning as well as afford professional exposure and preparation.

The first tool, "Fostering Alumni and Student Connections on LinkedIn," enables you to connect your students, colleagues, and staff with your alumni. The process is simple and straightforward. First, you create a LinkedIn group as part of your university's LinkedIn page. Then you ask all department members, including each new cohort of anthropology majors, to create or link their LinkedIn profiles to the group you just created. Next, you invite known alumni to join this group. As each cohort graduates, the proportion of alumni in the group grows. Anyone in the group can take advantage of the networking, discussions, and career opportunities posted.

30. Fostering Alumni and Student Connections on LinkedIn

Three other tools are client focused. They help you make connections with prospective client organizations, familiarize you and your students with issues these clients are facing, and suggest some best practices for interacting with clients. The tool "Making Connections with Local Organizations" recommends strategies you can use to network into organizations (e.g., introductions by someone you know, local organizations you can join). These connections represent an entry point for you and your students to gain valuable knowledge as well as work experience (e.g., project work, internships, consulting).

31. Making Connections with Local Organizations

The tool "How Do You Set up a Client-based Class Project?" introduces your students to project work sought by a client (e.g., business manager, nonprofit leader, municipal official). You and the client agree on the problem to be investigated by the students. Students gain experience in conducting research, compiling insights, and delivering a professional presentation to the client at the end of the term. Simultaneously, they learn to listen to the client and collaborate with their peers to complete the project. You can explore numerous client-based class projects on ACRN's website: https://anthrocareerready.net/for-instructors/class-projects/.

32. How Do You Set up a Client-based Class Project?

Interacting effectively with clients can be complicated so this tool will help: "Client Engagement Best Practices." If you or your students are interested in approaching a client about a consulting project, the interaction will play out across several stages: discovery and connection, relationship building, proposal and negotiation, project and client management, and project delivery and follow up. Conceptualizing the project as a partnership in which all parties benefit will get the project off to a good start. Typically, that advice translates into helping address a client problem in exchange for gaining access to the perspectives of client stakeholder groups (e.g., employees, customers, community members).

33. Client Engagement Best Practices

Establishing strong, healthy relationships with clients also can present short-term work experiences—that is, internship opportunities—for your students. A successful internship program represents a collaboration involving the student interns, their university supervisors, and their organizational hosts. This tool, "Setting Up an Internship Program," assumes your department does not yet have an infrastructure for coordinating internships. Consequently, it provides you with insights on the importance of internships for student development, strategies for setting up the internship program, as well as managing and promoting them. Of course, many anthropology departments work directly through their campus Career Services or Internship Office since they have years of experience in coordinating internships and employer contacts to offer.

34. Setting Up an Internship Program

ACRN has also produced a tool call the "Post-Internship Evaluation Guide." It is essential to assess how well your internship program is working from the point of view of the interns, their university supervisors, and their organizational hosts. (If your anthropology department has been working with campus Career Services or Internship Office, an internship evaluation may already be in place.) Our tool suggests questions to ask, methods for collecting the evaluation, as well as options for the question format (e.g., Likert scale, open-ended). In your analysis of the evaluations, prioritize the results by their urgency and importance.

35. Post-Internship Evaluation Guide

We end this section with a discussion of the value of campus career fairs. "Making Career Fairs Work for Anthropologists" offers two key applications for anthropology students. First, career fairs are an opportunity for conducting ethnographic research. Observation, interviews with recruiters, university staff, and other students, and participant observation can be carried out easily and seamlessly during these events. Students can debrief after to discuss what they documented and concluded from their investigation. Second, career fairs are also an opportunity for students to acquire information about specific organizations from recruiters. Students prepare their resumes in advance, learn about the characteristics recruiters seek in interns or new hires, and discuss the relevance of anthropology with these recruiters.

36. Making Career Fairs Work for Anthropologists

CHAPTER 3: SECURING ANTHROPOLOGY'S FUTURE

The time and effort needed to make decisions about departmental and coursework changes represent only part of your department's efforts. At this point you have made some decisions about the changes you plan to introduce into your department's culture and curriculum. Two follow-up questions include:

- How will those changes occur?

- How will those changes be sustained?

SOLVING THE CAREER READINESS PROBLEM

To address these questions, we return first to ACRN's emphasis on four interrelated concepts pertaining to career readiness: networking, communication, collaboration, and problem solving. Just as these concepts are useful in student preparation for the workplace, they are similarly instructive for departmental and instructor efforts pertaining to change. Taken together, these four concepts suggest both a response to the "How" questions and a potentially fruitful recipe for success.

Effective Problem Solving

Networking, communication, and collaboration are key foundational skills enabling effective problem solving, assuming interest and expertise (See Figure 7). While instructors routinely use these skills to advance their own careers, we suggest that they can apply these same skills to tackle key issues of the day such as rising expectations for career readiness.

Figure 7: Precursors to Effective Problem Solving

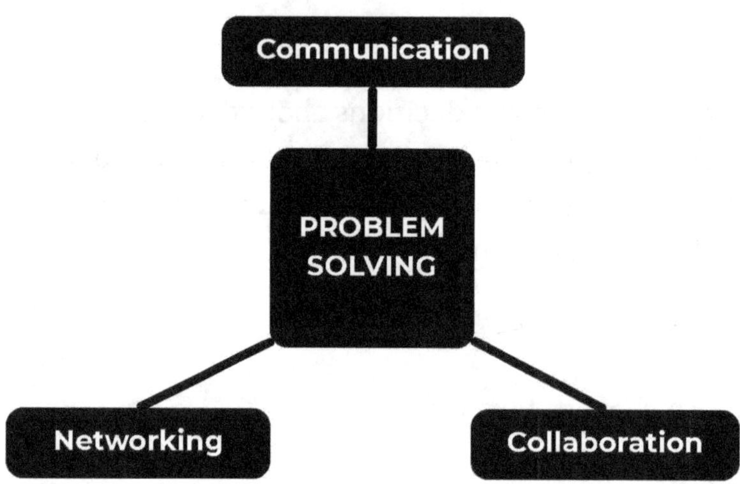

Addressing the career readiness issue likely involves different networks than the ones instructors typically cultivate. For example, during our DAI campus visits, anthropology professors often meet with members of Career Services for the first time. They usually express surprise and excitement about the range of services available to them and their students; they also indicate their appreciation for the connection with Career Services. This same pattern surfaces when instructors work with ACRN on a client-based class project. Instructors tend to approach a local organization with which they are familiar, though they may not know the specific contact person. A virtue of these novel connections is their potential to present new opportunities for both professors and students.

Using Selected Tools

It is also useful to consider these four concepts in relation to the tools presented earlier in the book. ACRN advocates developing new networks, extending existing forms of communication, and seeking new collaborations. Why? The answer to this question relates to the challenges affecting higher education, the workforce, and beyond—which require innovative solutions. The pressures on you and your department are too great to continue with the status quo. Career readiness must become a part of your teaching, just as it must become a part of student learning.

Many of the instructor tools relate directly to these four concepts. When you are contemplating how you might help your students learn the value of networking, these tools can be part of your "go to" set.

- [Fostering Alumni and Student Connections on LinkedIn](#)

- [Exploring Your Ecosystem to Expand Connections](#)

- [Making Connections with Local Organizations](#)

- [Informational Interviewing in the Classroom](#)

- [Making Career Fairs Work for Anthropologists](#)

- [Setting Up an Internship Program](#)

Making yourself understood is an important facet of communication, as is understanding information conveyed to you. This group of tools will not only help you shape the messaging for your students, but also acquaint them with forms of communication used in the workplace and in society.

- [A Career Ready Curriculum](#)

- [Drafting Your Anthropology Department Roadmap](#)

- [A Better ANTH 101](#)

- [Introducing Anthropology in a First-Year Course](#)

- [Promoting Courses with a Dash of Pop Culture](#)

- [Bringing Anthropological Practice into the Classroom](#)

- [Teaching with Blogposts](#)

- [Teaching with Op-Eds](#)

Listening is a fundamental element of collaboration, whether with your anthropology colleagues, alumni from your program, or prospective clients. These tools will assist you in creating new collaborations for and with your students.

- [Addressing Instructor Concerns about Career Readiness](#)

- [Building Department-Alumni Connections](#)

- [How Do You Set up a Client-based Class Project?](#)

- <u>Launching and Sustaining a Community Advisory Board</u>

- <u>Client Engagement Best Practices</u>

The fourth concept, problem solving, is associated with several tools for identifying and diagnosing issues, as well as revealing pathways for potential action. While "The Departmental Advisory Initiative" targets career readiness specifically, the remaining tools can be applied to any relevant stakeholder issue—including those of your colleagues or students.

- <u>The Departmental Advisory Initiative</u>

- <u>Finding Clarity with Concept Maps</u>

- <u>Putting Force Field Analysis to Work</u>

- <u>Using Brainstorming for Collaborative Problem Solving</u>

- <u>Making Group Decisions through Discussion</u>

DEVELOPING AND IMPLEMENTING YOUR CAREER READINESS PLAN

Next, we turn to the specific career readiness changes that you and your colleagues have agreed to undertake. Developing an implementation plan helps you to list and track your goals and objectives in an effective and timely manner. "Creating an Implementation Plan for Action" shows you how to craft a plan that can be customized to your specific circumstances.

<u>37. Creating an Implementation Plan for Action</u>

Your plan will include objective statements that are "SMART," that is, Specific, Measurable, Appropriate, Realistic, and Time-bound. For each objective, you decide on the activities you plan to do, any resources needed, the actors involved, the timeframe, indicators to measure success, the data or information for verifying your indicators, and the key assumptions linked to your objectives. Thus, you set the terms and the performance metrics.

Your focus now turns to accomplishing the goals and objectives laid out in the plan. The four concepts—networking, communication, collaboration, and problem solving—will work to your advantage once again. As the work gets underway, outreach to new contacts, frequent communication between you, your colleagues, and other stakeholders, and a spirit of teamwork position you for success. Yet, success is also contingent on the work of the collective, not just a few career readiness champions. You strive for outcomes that represent a completed rather than partial or limited effort.

Addressing the Obstacles

Your version of planned change is likely to collide with obstacles as the work gets underway. For example, some instructors may be less willing to contribute fully to the plan: they may not be convinced of the need to change how they teach. Alternatively, an entire program may be unable to support the plan due to new, urgent priorities (e.g., shifting tenure and promotion policies, major funding losses). While individual resistance and departmental crises may lead to distinctive responses, both are illustrative of problems begging for solutions.

How might anthropology departments deal with obstacles generally? Here are a few suggested strategies, though many others may emerge from one of the problem-solving tools described earlier:

- Settling on a "lead" person for each objective not only helps distribute the workload but also generates some pressure to complete the task.

- Prioritizing those matters over which you have some degree of control is a strategy that makes good sense.

- Holding regular progress updates on the career readiness plan can help to reinforce agreed-upon expectations, even during periods of uncertainty.

- Leveraging your stakeholders for helpful insights, connections, and/or advice that is relevant to your situation can make a challenging situation simpler and easier.

- Activating specific positive processes associated with your department's culture (e.g., aligning with other social science disciplines, learning from past crises) to support the implementation plan works to mitigate the obstacles you face.

- Agreeing to suspend implementation tasks *briefly* while a) assessing fallout from a crisis and b) managing the transition may help you and your colleagues concentrate fully on career readiness following a plan to address a crisis.

Sustaining Change

One of the biggest problems surrounding academic change is the question of the sustainability of effort. All too often, changes begun in one year are discarded a year or two later, and whatever progress has been made then evaporates. If a change is not working, then of course it is necessary to address the issue. However, if something is working, then it is equally necessary to keep things going. Otherwise, the time, effort and money put into getting things off the ground have been largely wasted.

Dimensions of Sustainability

"Sustainability" has a few different dimensions. We emphasize three of them here: transfer, resource flows, and management capacity. For each, relevant questions are posed to help you integrate and maintain a spotlight on career readiness in your department. Our goal for you is to position you to be as successful as possible in sustaining career readiness over time.

<u>Transfer</u>	If activities will be "handed over," is there a plan in place to do so? Have people been designated to take on the work? Is there a timetable for handover? Is any additional training needed to ensure a smooth handover? Is there a contingency plan in place?
<u>Resource Flows</u>	What resources (e.g., money, time, space, personnel) will be required to keep things going? Where will these resources come from? How much is available locally, and how much is dependent on outside bodies?
<u>Management Capacity</u>	Will your department's organizational capacities be sufficient to sustain changes at an acceptable level? If not, how do you plan to improve them? What aspects of the program will be run locally? Who will be responsible?

Selected Sustainability Strategies

Typically, new initiatives have champions who take on most of the heavy lifting. When these individuals leave, or find new interests, things often fall apart. There are many ways to promote sustainability in new endeavors; we cover several of them here. Specific sustainability strategies should be discussed within your department. Then, decisions need to be made to put in place one or more of these strategies at the outset of the academic change process.

Fundraising: Typically, most anthropology departments do not consider fundraising to be either part of their work or something the department is particularly good at (securing grants excluded). Yet, having outside connections or exploring new ones can provide welcomed resources. For example, fundraising could make it possible for students to accept unpaid internships and still be compensated, or to provide the necessary funding for students to participate in a field school where they would have the opportunity to learn and practice new skills.

Foundations are often the easiest donors to identify and approach since you can research them via Candid's *Foundation Directory*, available online (https://candid.org, accessed January 12, 2026). However, foundations are diverse in size and focus, so it is important to ensure that there is a strong fit between your department's goals and their funding priorities. With cuts to U.S. federal funding, foundations have been experiencing a significant rise in demand leading to more competition for limited funds. Unless you have a relationship with a program officer at a particular foundation, it may be difficult to "stand out from the crowd."

Consequently, it is more important than ever to identify and foster individual donors—your alumni, retired faculty, local businesspeople, or enthusiasts about the work that your departmental colleagues and students do. When you are ready to approach a donor, follow the guidance in ACRN's "Keys to Fundraising Success" tool, which also appears in the *Career Tools for Anthropology* workbook.

Alumni Networking: Many departments do not reach out to their alumni, some because they have lost contact with them. (Earlier, we stressed using the tool "Fostering Alumni & Student Connections on LinkedIn" to address this issue.) It is an excellent idea to keep in touch with your alumni because they can provide you with needed resources.

One resource, of course, is financial. A second is intern and job placements. And a third resource is insight into what practitioners actually do. Alumni are willing to offer career tips and counsel to you and your students, among many other possible forms of assistance. By inviting your alumni to engage with your department, you stay on top of trends in the field, which will be helpful to you in your teaching and useful to your students in their internship and job searches.

Advisory Boards: Like alumni, advisory boards can be a source of funding, of networking, and of up-to-date information. They can also provide you with insight, advice, and warnings.

Advisory boards are usually composed of organizational and community members; alumni may serve on them as well. Extending strategic invitations to a mix of innovative thinkers, entrepreneurs, and subject matter experts will provide you with diverse and relevant input for your department.

Tenure and promotion reform: Recruitment, promotion and tenure systems at most U.S. institutions militate against instructors with interests in practice and application. These procedures are one of the main reasons that it has been so difficult for the discipline to respond to changing external conditions and expectations. Although changing such policies for an entire university would be a formidable task, it is entirely possible to do so at the level of the department, provided the will is there.

Changing the pattern of pressures and incentives would make it much easier to engage in curricular innovation and change, and to maintain such changes once they are made. Introducing practice as a recognized and rewarded feature of your department also sends important messages to students about the value of applying anthropology in the workplace, in the community, and in society generally.

Communicating across Institutions: U.S. higher education institutions are remarkably siloed; attending a national academic meeting once or twice a year does not do much to overcome the silos and improve communication, collaboration, and dissemination of lessons learned. Consider setting up an informal network of your peer institutions at a national or regional level. Use videoconferencing to meet from time to time to exchange information and experiences, as well as seek advice. Although institutions are unique, they have remarkably similar problems so that what works well for one may very well work for another.

ACRN has just launched the DAI Forum, a discussion group of past and current DAI participating departments. The Forum is designed to improve the cross-fertilization of career readiness ideas—both successful strategies as well as the challenges programs have faced. Our plan is to hold the Forum twice yearly for 90 minutes. We will designate a general topic for each session which will be moderated. We anticipate that the information exchanged in these sessions will encourage programs to continue to experiment and transform long after they have completed the DAI program and gone on to integrate newer forms of career readiness into their curriculum and departmental programming.

CONCLUSION

You are preparing students to face a rapidly changing job market and world. Anthropology offers a unique and powerful set of perspectives and methods for discovery, analysis, understanding, and targeted action. Career readiness will allow your students to adapt to new contexts, identify and tackle new problems, and become agents of change in their communities.

In this book, we have provided a range of tools and techniques to help departments—and individual instructors—respond to student needs, to outside challenges, and to the exciting opportunities which exist for the application of what we know and learn. You have the opportunity to prepare yourselves and your students to address the problems of today and the future. We encourage you to innovate and share your successes back with us and the larger discipline.

Each department will change and develop in its own unique way; hopefully this book will play a positive role in supporting the changes that you initiate. We, like you, are engaged in an ongoing effort to improve what we do as anthropologists. We welcome your suggestions for new topics and well as for changes and improvements to the material we have presented here.

DEPARTMENT AND INSTRUCTOR TOOLS

1. Your Career Ready Department Checklist

Elizabeth K. Briody

Anthropology Department members often ask how they might integrate career readiness into their department's programming. This tool contains checklists of activities which can be carried out by the Department as a whole. Institutionalizing career readiness is essential to Department sustainability, particularly during times of high uncertainty and upheaval. Formalizing the process in the Bachelor's, Master's, and PhD programs enables students to connect academic theory to practical applications and enhance their career outcomes.

Why Checklists?

Checklists have many purposes:

- **Communicate the value** of career readiness to students, prospective students, administrators, and alumni

- **Demonstrate alignment** with university-wide initiatives on career readiness

- **Measure progress over time** in institutionalizing career readiness activities and assessing program goals

- **Propose and secure new criteria** for tenure and promotion

Department Checklist

This Department Checklist has the potential to build career readiness into Department culture and help you bridge the gap between the Department and the world beyond. Practitioners, alumni, and community members all play critical roles.

The Department Checklist contains two parts—Engagement with Industry, Nonprofit, Government Employees, and Career Readiness Activities. Most of the links are to the Instructor Tools on the ACRN website.

Instructions

Use this table to identify the number of times career readiness activities were sponsored by the Department during the last term. Referencing the scale below, score and track progress each term. After each assessment, review the Department Checklist to set expanded goals for incorporating career readiness into Department programming in the future. For example, certain career events can be built into the Department calendar on a repeating basis (e.g., career panel in fall term, practitioner-led methodology workshop in spring term).

Urgent Need for Career Readiness (Score = 0)

- No career readiness activities in place

Limited Career Readiness (Score = 1-3)

- Occasional alumni guest speakers
- Capstone products include a resume and portfolio
- Career panel held three years ago

Moderate Career Readiness (Score = 4-7)

- Two courses carry out client-based class projects each term
- New professionalization course taught once
- Department roadmap being created
- Department LinkedIn Group launched with invitations sent to several alumni

Robust Career Readiness (Score = 8+)

- Numerous career activities integrated into 80% of semester coursework
- A Department career panel and practitioner workshop each term
- Required UG and grad student participation in certain Career Services events
- All UG students reliably secure at least one internship

Engagement with Industry, Nonprofit, and Government Employees (e.g., Practitioners, Alumni)	Times during the last term?
• as guest speakers and/or panelists	
• as workshop presenters	
• as part of the network for internships and jobs	
• as internship supervisors	
• as members of a Community Advisory Board	
• Other (specify)	
Total Activities	

Career Readiness Activities	Times during the last term?
Create a LinkedIn Group for your Department	
Get all students, instructors, and staff to create their LinkedIn profiles and join this LinkedIn Group	
Invite all known alumni to join this LinkedIn Group	
Establish the career ready curriculum as a Department priority	
Develop a relationship with your alumni as a way to assist your students (e.g., with mentoring, internships, job contacts)	
Build relationships with campus Career Services, disseminating their resources and events to students	
Work closely with campus Career Services to identify possible internship placements for UG and graduate students	
Require an internship for UG students	
Require an internship for graduate students	
Reach out to local organizations to benefit your students and these organizations (e.g., client-based class projects, service learning, internships)	
Draft a Department Roadmap for your Bachelor's, Master's and/or PhD programs	
Create a career page on your Department website, posting profiles of alumni careers, relevant career-related programming sponsored by the Department, skill-building activities, and internship opportunities	
Establish a Community Advisory Board	
Other (specify)	
Total Activities	
Grand Total of Career Readiness Activities	

2. The Departmental Advisory Initiative

Elizabeth K. Briody

The Departmental Advisory Initiative (DAI) is an ACRN service designed to improve student career readiness in Anthropology Departments. Often, anthropology instructors have had limited exposure to careers beyond the academy and the problem-solving expectations associated with them. ACRN's DAI facilitators work directly with instructors to help them build individual and departmental capacity to prepare students for careers in industry, non-profits, and government.

Why was DAI launched?

The initiative began in 2023 in response to the:

- Lack of attention to career preparation which characterized many Anthropology Departments

- Problems experienced by many anthropology graduates in finding jobs beyond the academy

- Increasing pressures felt by universities to ensure student career preparation.

ACRN leadership believed that it could improve student career readiness by working with Departments on a customized plan that would be implemented over one year.

What is the DAI process?

Four distinct activities are associated with DAI. The first two involve data gathering, the third entails data analysis, and the fourth emphasizes action—the execution of an implementation plan drawn up by the Department in consultation with ACRN. These four activities are similar to the work in which many practitioners typically engage: research, evaluation, program planning and the implementation of change.

1. DAI Initiated with Application

Departments demonstrate their interest in DAI by completing a short application. In addition to basic Department information, the application includes the key goals and issues the Department would like to address.

Once the application is received, ACRN facilitators schedule a call with the Department contact person, often the Chair; other Department members may also participate. This discussion is an opportunity for both ACRN and the Department to ask questions regarding the application and the ACRN process, respectively.

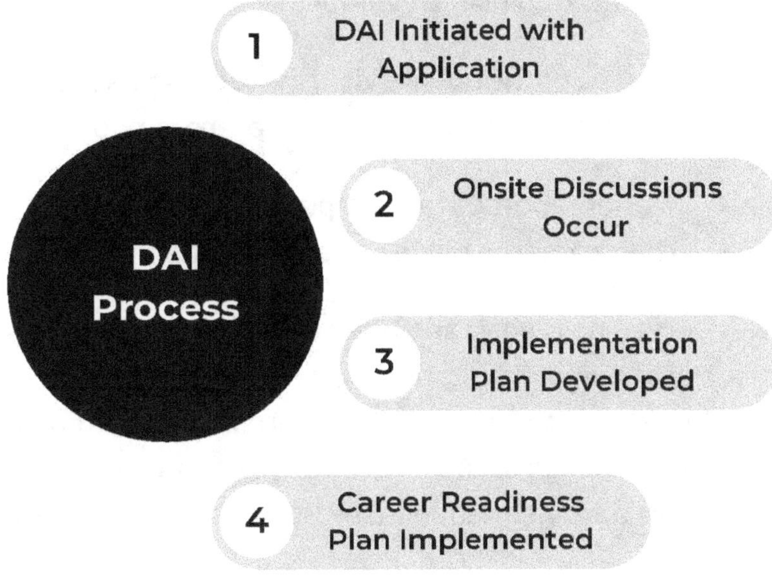

2. Onsite Discussions Occur

At a time convenient for the Department, two ACRN facilitators visit the campus for two to three days to work with Department members intensively. An opening presentation, to which all are invited, focuses on the changing academic context as well as ACRN's resources and services.

The Department forms a designated Working Group of six to eight members. Together with ACRN facilitators, the group engages in a SWOT (i.e., Strengths, Weaknesses, Opportunities, and Threats) exercise and a survey of the local organizational ecosystem. Then, ACRN facilitators conduct a design workshop focused on Department priorities; career readiness ideas and possible activities are identified.

All Department members are invited to the closing session. ACRN facilitators offer actionable recommendations for the Department's career readiness implementation plan. The facilitators actively solicit feedback from Department members, integrating it into documents that will be sent back to the Department after the campus visit concludes.

3. Implementation Plan Developed

Within a week of the on-site visit, the facilitators pass along all presentations and notes. The Working Group uses this material to prepare two new documents:

- A brief report of the campus visit
- Their career readiness implementation plan.

Career readiness goals and objectives that the Department intends to accomplish are at the heart of the implementation plan. Many of these goals pertain to curriculum while others may be related to issues such as enrollment, outreach to alumni, engagement with Career Services on campus, and networking with area organizations. A Gantt chart, a timeline with objectives arranged sequentially by quarter, is incorporated into the plan.

4. Career Readiness Changes Implemented

ACRN facilitators meet virtually with the Working Group once every quarter over the next 12 months. The purpose of these meetings is to follow up with the Department on their implementation progress and serve as a source of support to them. One year is sufficient time to achieve most, if not all the goals, included in the plan. When the year is over, the Department receives a DAI certificate of completion from ACRN.

Who are the facilitators?

Just as ACRN is practitioner-led, so too is DAI. All facilitators have decades of experience in the private, nonprofit, and public sectors. Most have worked both in the U.S. and abroad. They recognize the importance of context and anthropological subfield in shaping student career preparation.

How have Departments responded to DAI?

Participants have expressed strong, positive views of DAI. They have indicated benefitting from the brainstorming and discussions with their colleagues in a structured, moderated format. The on-site visit and follow-up virtual meetings allow them to set aside time dedicated to this effort.

Participants have indicated that they can express their ideas, reflect upon options, voice concerns, and present alternatives. They have pointed out that DAI facilitators draw from their own work experiences as practitioners and from the experiences of other DAI Departments. Such comparisons often stimulate innovative thinking among Department members, grounded in their own university context.

Perhaps most importantly, the quarterly follow-up meetings present opportunities for each Department to "stay on track" and hold themselves accountable. The specific goals and objectives of their implementation plan is a visual reminder of what they agreed to do. As such, it is a strong motivator for action fostering career readiness.

What are the costs?

ACRN is a network that is entirely based on volunteers. The only cost for a participating Department is travel costs for a campus visit by two facilitators. Sources of funding include:

- **Department and/or university funds**

    o While on campus, ACRN leaders can deliver a public seminar/university lecture which often frees up internal funding

- **External grants**

- **DAI Award:** Sponsored by COPAA of the Society for Applied Anthropology (SfAA) and the American Anthropological Association (AAA), $1,000 Awards are available through at least 2028. To be eligible, the Department must either belong to AAA's Departmental Services Program, or the submitter must be a member of SfAA. Find the DAI application at https://anthrocareerready.net/for-instructors/departmental-advisory-initiative. Upload your completed DAI application by **December 1**. You will be notified by **January 15** and will welcome the facilitators to your campus in **spring**.

What are the results?

Each Anthropology Department/Program is unique which means that the outcomes pertaining to their implementation plan will be unique. However, all participants should complete DAI with the following:

- A <u>Career Ready Curriculum</u> that prepares students for the workplace

- A deeper understanding of their organizational ecosystem

- An expanded network of alumni, practitioners, and community members.

Each Department also leaves with the tools and resources to continue this work beyond the initial year and to respond to ongoing changes as needed. Most importantly, their graduates should be able to articulate the value and relevance of anthropology to employers, colleagues, and others in their lives and go on to careers where they can apply their anthropological training in solving problems and making change in the world.

3. Using SWOT to Prepare for Change

Riall W. Nolan

SWOT is an acronym which stands for Strengths, Weaknesses, Opportunities and Threats. A SWOT analysis is a way to analyze an organization, such as your department, in terms of internal and external factors. It can help you decide on strategic areas of focus which might affect future courses of action. Because this technique is both simple and effective, SWOT has been used by organizations of all types, for decades.

There are several reasons why conducting a SWOT analysis might be a good idea for your department. First, it enables you collectively to assemble and discuss important information about who you are. Second, SWOT helps you understand key aspects of the environment surrounding your department. Identifying and understanding these external forces can be particularly important in situations of rapid change. Third, and most importantly, it is useful when you are contemplating some form of change, or new activity, often in response to changes in the greater environment. SWOT draws your attention to possibilities and choices and can help you chart a way forward. In other words, it works as a problem-structuring tool.

Conceptualizing SWOT

A SWOT analysis helps you relate your department's key characteristics to the salient features of the surrounding environment. A simple matrix is used in which strengths and weaknesses are internal to your department while opportunities and threats are present in the external environment surrounding the department.

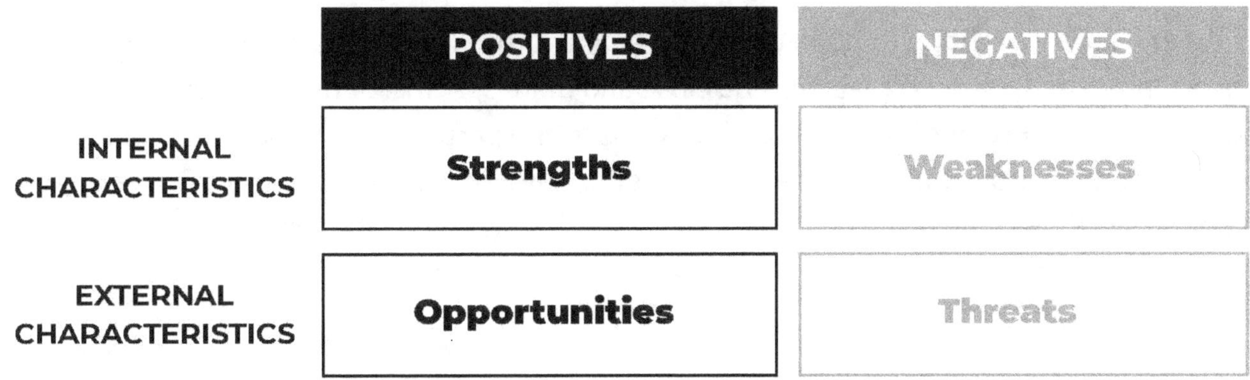

The SWOT analysis positions you to examine these strengths, weaknesses, opportunities, and threats in relation to one another, allows you to map the interactions between them, and in the process, helps identify strategic issues for the department's focus.

The SWOT process consists of four steps:

1. Listing opportunities and threats

2. Listing strengths and weaknesses

3. Analyzing interactions between factors

4. Choosing issues for action.

1. Listing Opportunities and Threats

SWOT begins with an inventory of the threats and opportunities in your department's external environment followed by a listing of your department's internal strengths and weaknesses. Studies have shown that rather than conducting an internal analysis first, departments should start instead with identifying external opportunities and threats. Understanding the larger context in which your department operates can motivate you to think more broadly about which internal factors are relevant as well as avoid the risk of an overly internal or insular focus. In other words, taking an outside-in approach can help you uncover internal factors you may not have even considered.

To prepare for a SWOT, ask department members to jot down their views of the strengths, weaknesses, opportunities and threats before you meet. Then, conduct your SWOT analysis live, as a group, in a <u>brainstorming session</u>. Keep discussion and evaluation to a minimum as you gather all the input.

The same factor might be both an opportunity and a threat; factors can be listed more than once. Opportunities and threats may be close and quite specific, or more general and distant. List anything that seems important and relevant to the participants. It may also help to think of threats and opportunities in terms of overall categories. One common framework for doing this is PEST: Political, Economic, Social and Technological factors.

Here is a fictional example of a list of external opportunities and threats:

OUTSIDE OPPORTUNITIES	OUTSIDE THREATS
<ul><li>Readiness within university for change</li><li>Room for growth into new areas of teaching and research</li><li>Strong external demand for our courses</li><li>Potential partnerships with local organizations</li><li>Local opportunities in health, criminology, conservation, and aging</li><li>Potential for alumni relationships</li><li>Unexplored fundraising avenues</li></ul>	<ul><li>Federal budget freezes and firings</li><li>Decrease in state support</li><li>Ignorance of / Low public opinion of anthropology</li><li>Rising costs of operations/tuition</li><li>Low Return on Investment (ROI) for graduate program</li><li>Attacks on Diversity, Equity, and Inclusion (DEI)</li><li>Current university business model</li><li>Disciplinary decline overall</li><li>Inadequate preparation of new students</li><li>Pressure to keep student numbers high</li></ul>

2. Listing Strengths and Weaknesses

Next, explore your department's internal strengths and weaknesses. Again, a specific factor might be a strength as well as a weakness. Do not try to judge or prioritize the strength of these factors; at this stage it is more important to list them all. Do not settle for broad or vague terms. Instead, be as specific as possible in describing each factor.

Here is a list of internal strengths and weaknesses:

DEPARTMENT STRENGTHS	DEPARTMENT WEAKNESSES
<ul><li>Positive relationship with administration</li><li>Focus on students</li><li>High student evaluations</li><li>Good climate/morale</li><li>Strong faculty</li><li>Good physical facilities</li><li>Collaborative spirit</li><li>Good reputation</li><li>Wide range of activities</li><li>Research and teaching in line with university aims</li></ul>	<ul><li>Too much to do</li><li>Gaps in course coverage</li><li>Small size of faculty</li><li>Lack of overall strategic plan</li><li>Losses of faculty members over time</li><li>Pressures on class size</li><li>Lack of stability in administration</li><li>Budget constraints</li><li>Departmental leadership uncertainties</li></ul>

3. Analyzing Interactions Between Factors

Once you have sufficient information about the internal and external environments, arrange the lists in a way to help you understand their interactions and their possible significance for you.

Begin by listing all the factors identified in one big table.

	POSITIVES	NEGATIVES
INTERNAL	• Positive relationship with administration • Focus on students • High student evaluations • Good climate/morale • Strong faculty • Good physical facilities • Collaborative spirit • Good reputation • Wide range of activities • Research and teaching in line with university aims	• Too much to do • Gaps in course coverage • Small size of faculty • Lack of overall strategic plan • Losses of faculty members over time • Pressures on class size • Lack of stability in administration • Budget constraints • Departmental leadership uncertainties
EXTERNAL	• Readiness within university for change • Room for growth into new areas of teaching and research • Strong external demand for our courses • Potential partnerships with local organizations • Local opportunities in health, criminology, conservation, and aging • Potential for alumni relationships • Unexplored fundraising avenues	• Federal budget freezes and firings • Decrease in state support • Ignorance of / Low public opinion of anthropology • Rising costs of operations/tuition • Attacks on DEI • Low ROI for graduate program • Current university business model • Disciplinary decline overall • Inadequate preparation of new students • Pressure to keep student numbers high

Next, juxtapose these various factors to identify salient linkages between internal strengths and weaknesses and external threats and opportunities. Here is an example, using the factors identified.

<table>
<tr><td>What should we be paying attention to now?</td><td>OPPORTUNITIES

• Readiness within university for change
• Room for growth into new areas of teaching and research
• Strong external demand for our courses
• Potential partnerships with local organizations
• Local opportunities in health, criminology, conservation, and aging
• Potential for alumni relationships
• Unexplored fundraising avenues</td><td>THREATS

• Federal budget freezes and firings
• Decrease in state support
• Ignorance of / Low public opinion of anthropology
• Rising costs of operations/tuition
• Attacks on DEI
• Low ROI for graduate program
• Current university business model
• Disciplinary decline overall
• Inadequate preparation of new students
• Pressure to keep student numbers high</td></tr>
<tr><td>STRENGTHS

• Positive relationship with administration
• Focus on students
• High student evaluations
• Good climate/morale
• Strong faculty
• Good physical facilities
• Collaborative spirit
• Good reputation
• Wide range of activities
• Research and teaching in line with university aims</td><td>Predominant Capabilities</td><td>Mobilization</td></tr>
<tr><td>WEAKNESSES

• Too much to do
• Gaps in course coverage
• Small size of faculty
• Lack of overall strategic plan
• Losses of faculty members over time
• Pressures on class size
• Lack of stability in administration
• Budget constraints
• Departmental leadership uncertainties</td><td>Investment or Divestment</td><td>Damage Control</td></tr>
</table>

This juxtaposition will direct your attention to those features of your situation which may require some work and which provide possible answers to the question "What should we be paying attention to now?

Strengths, weaknesses, opportunities and threats combine in four main ways:

- **Opportunities** and **strengths** combine to generate a set of **predominant capabilities**, where your department's strengths respond well to one or more opportunities in your surrounding environment. Your department excels in this quadrant.

- **Opportunities** and **weaknesses** combine to produce situations where your department may want to decide either to **invest** in certain activities (to take advantage of the opportunities) or **divest** itself of some present activities (to lighten the load and/or avoid future problems).

- **Threats** and **strengths** combine to produce situations where your department's existing or past experience, skills, or resources might need to be **mobilized** to produce positive outcomes or avoid negative ones.

- Finally, **threats** and **weaknesses** combine to create situations where **damage control** may be necessary to avoid making a bad situation worse.

4. Choosing Issues for Action

To conclude the SWOT analysis, the department makes some strategic decisions about which ideas to follow up on, and how. Each of the four sets of combinations will probably generate several possibilities. Although you are not obliged to pursue any of them, some may be too good to pass up, while others—perhaps in the damage control quadrant—may be of a fairly urgent nature. Obviously, you will not be able to take up all the issues identified in a SWOT analysis at once. Additionally, you may not have the resources to work on more than a few, in any case.

To make choices, rank the various options, following these guidelines.

Issues in any of the cells of the matrix can be chosen. Although it is tempting to look first at items appearing under comparative advantage (where you are strongest) or under damage control (where you are weakest), you should consider the items appearing under both investment/divestment and mobilization.

You might rank the issues in terms of your ability as a department or organization to influence them. Which problems, for example, could most likely be ameliorated by your group? Which issues might be influenced, but perhaps not completely addressed by your team? And which issues seem to lie largely outside your control or influence? You should probably stay away from issues that you cannot affect appreciably with your available skills and resources.

Then develop some simple criteria to help you sort out the remaining issues. Here are some guiding principles that might be helpful.

- **Relevance**: Is this issue of significant concern to your department? How urgent, severe, or important is this issue compared with the others? Will addressing this issue help you address other issues? What would happen if you did nothing?

- **Change**: What happens if you address the issue successfully? Who wins and who loses? What else might happen if you make changes? What other issues might be affected? Will your solutions be lasting or temporary?

- **Learning**: If you address this issue, what is the potential for departmental learning and for departmental capacity building? If you learn useful lessons, do they have "spin-offs" to other situations?

- **Level of Effort**: How difficult will this issue be to address in a satisfactory manner? Do you have the time, skills and/or resources? Do you need others to help you? Can you get the help you need?

- **Process**: Do you have the skill and the experience to manage any efforts in which you engage? Do you understand enough about what may be required? If you do not have the required skill, can you learn it or do you need to find it elsewhere?

These criteria are arbitrary. Use them as a starting point to make up your own set. Consultation and involvement with all members of your department—and possibly with outside stakeholders—will be essential to the development of a shared and workable framework for preparation for change.

4. Exploring Your Ecosystem to Expand Connections

Riall W. Nolan

Every department has a unique ecosystem or surrounding environment within which its activities unfold. This ecosystem has three distinct dimensions, all of which have importance for how your department works. These dimensions are distinguished one from the other based on the amount of influence your department has over them.

Dimensions of Your Ecosystem

You have almost total control over certain aspects of your working environment and virtually no influence over other parts of it. However, understanding these dimensions of your environment, and their different parts, positions you to operate as effectively as possible.

- Your **inner environment** contains those elements that are directly under the control of the department and/or its members. Offices and office space, labs, personnel, equipment, and budget are some of the elements you manage.

- Immediately beyond the inner environment is what we call the **negotiated environment**. It represents the elements of your surroundings which are in close contact with your department. These parts of your environment are outside your direct control, but they have an influence on your activities. Among these elements are your university administration, regional and national scholarly organizations, journals and publishers, funders of all sorts, and potential partners. Furthermore, although they can influence you, you can also influence them. You are in more or less constant interaction with this aspect of your environment.

- The **outer environment** also affects what you do inside the department, although you have little if any influence over it. This environment includes such elements as the national economy, the political and legal system, the climate, topography, and natural resources of the area.

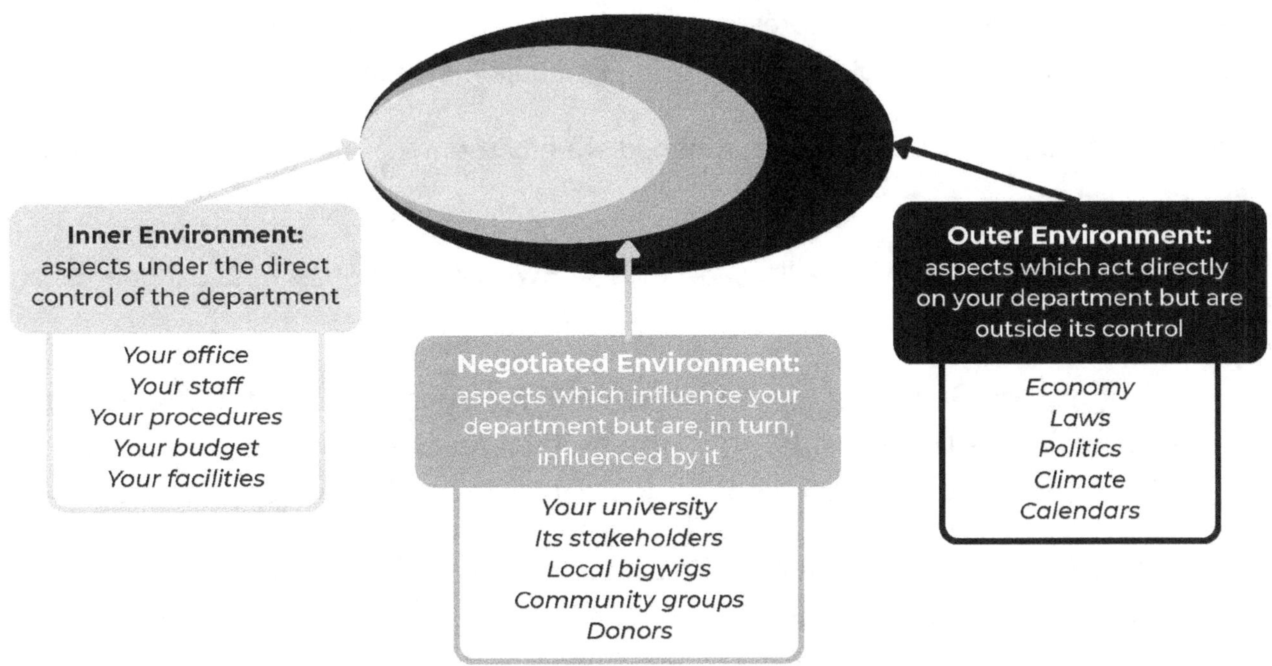

All elements of the ecosystem are important, but not all of them may be known or well understood by people in the department. Planning strategies should recognize these three dimensions of the ecosystem and monitor any significant changes in them which may affect your department.

Putting Your Ecosystem to Work

In addition to providing a framework for identifying various factors influencing a department's operation, examining the ecosystem can also help a department identify potential sources of support in the form of resources, information, or networks. ACRN's Departmental Advisory Initiative incorporates an exercise for departmental participants in which key elements of the ecosystem are identified with these forms of support in mind. We look first at groups and organizations on campus, and then move outward to the community and beyond. We call this an asset analysis.

Analyzing Your Assets

You may know that a needs analysis emphasizes aspects of the environment that are lacking with a focus on problems; it tends to see people as clients or consumers. In contrast, an

asset analysis explores what is present with a focus on existing strengths, experience, resources and potential; it looks at opportunities to build partnerships with people.

Various assets are associated with your immediate environment and well beyond it. Assets include:

- **Individuals**: People with skills, capacities, knowledge, resources, and experience are among your assets.

- **Associations**: Groups of people, organized for specific purposes, are based in communities. All communities have dozens if not hundreds of different associations, of all types. Other associations are regional, national and international in scope.

- **Institutions and organizations**: These entities include government offices and institutions (e.g., schools) as well as businesses and services of various types. They exist in all communities and at a wider scale.

- **Networks**: Connections may be informal or quasi-formal within and outside your community. They may not be highly visible, but they exist everywhere and are important.

- **Past knowledge and experience**: All communities have a history including their individual and collective experiences, accomplishments, stories, and other elements. As a result, there is an important store of knowledge among people about how things work.

- **Physical assets**: Community assets may be public or private and include such features as land, water, buildings, parks, and transportation infrastructure. All of them are important for how people live.

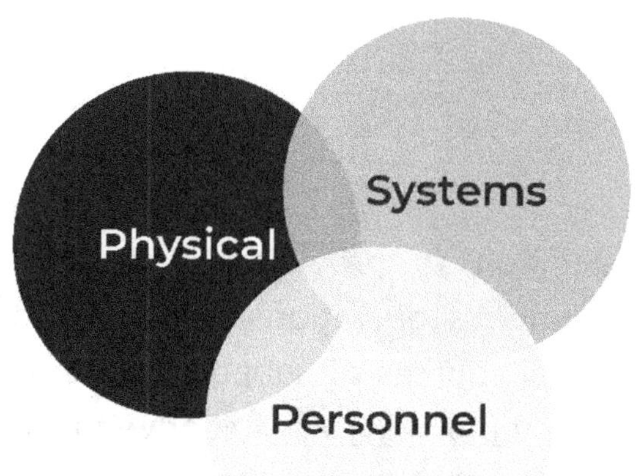

A Framework for Exploring Your Ecosystem

As you begin to explore your ecosystem, a framework is helpful to guide your enquiry. There are many reasons to investigate your ecosystem including:

- identifying sources of <u>internships</u> and jobs for students
- gaining valuable experience with <u>client-based class projects</u>
- research and consulting opportunities for faculty
- influential and knowledgeable individuals in your area who can be advocates, <u>advisors</u> and supporters.

Here is one example of a framework for exploring your surrounding community.

Who are the different groups?	Stakeholder groups can include local nonprofits, communities, businesses, interest groups, individuals, officials, and institutions, among others.
What influence and assets do they have?	These groups have varied and multiple interests, skills, and resources and may be beneficiaries, gatekeepers, informants, controllers, funders, legislators, subscribers, and employers, among others.
What might they need or want from you?	Stakeholders may have needs and expectations that differ from your department and its programs. Some groups might know very little about you. Others may have inaccurate or skewed impressions of what you do. Still other groups may face challenges or issues with which you could help and may be interested in learning from you.
What might they contribute?	Stakeholders have a variety of resources which might be made available to you. For example, these resources might include knowledge, skills, money, participation, materials, political support, advocacy, networking, and advice.
What more might you need to know?	Working effectively with stakeholders necessitates learning more about them, such as their composition, size, history, personalities, leadership structure, rules, preferences, linkages, and positions on issues, among other aspects.

5. Analyzing Stakeholders to Build Support

Riall W. Nolan

An important part of making any new departmental initiative successful involves understanding who may be involved in what you are planning, how they might be affected, and how they might react. Referred to as stakeholders, these people have influence over your plans and activities. They may be members of your department and/or other groups or individuals outside the department. Understanding and managing your stakeholders is particularly important in big departmental initiatives, such as revamping your curriculum, adding tracks, courses or degrees, and partnering with another department, university, or organization.

Stakeholder Help or Hindrance?

Stakeholders can include any group or individual with the power to help, hinder, or otherwise influence what you are planning to do. Stakeholder groups have both interest in your project and resources which could be applied or withheld. Consequently, it is important to uncover and understand those interests and resources, find ways of fitting them into your planning, and manage your stakeholder relationships throughout the process. Not all stakeholders are going to be supportive. Stakeholders can be arranged along a rough continuum, according to their degree of enthusiasm or support for your efforts.

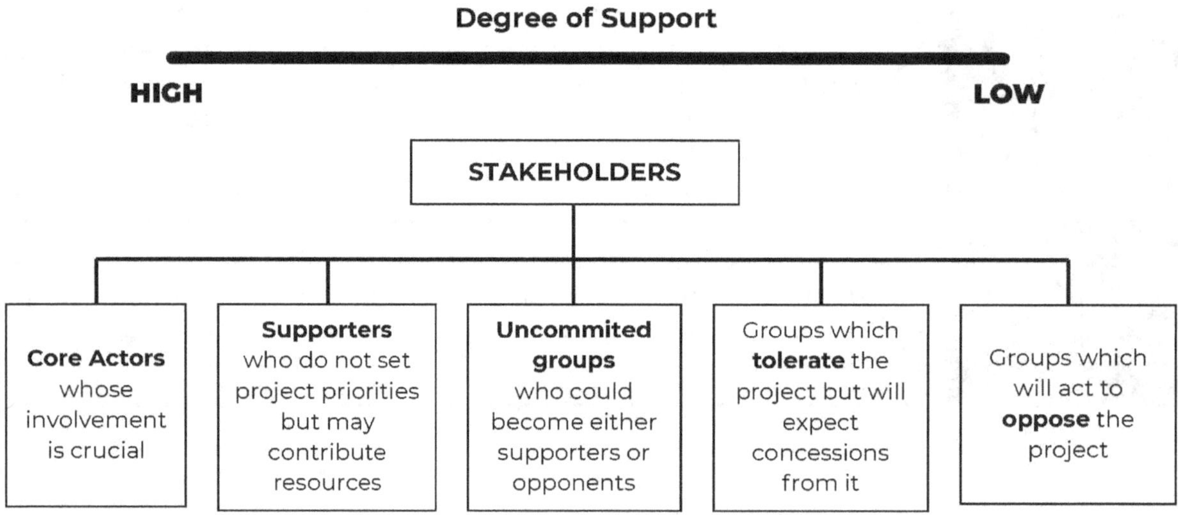

While it is important to know who your core actors or champions are, it is equally important to identify groups or individuals who may never be on board with you. Groups which expect concessions from you will need to be dealt with carefully. Most instructors consider their "buying-in" as agreeing not to oppose something, rather than lending support to it—which may not necessarily be what you need or want.

Process

1. As you identify your stakeholders, specify what power or influence they have. Gather information on:

- The basis of their influence (e.g., votes, money, knowledge, authority)

- The scope of their influence (i.e., in what areas can they be influential)

- The amount of influence that might be applied

- How their influence might be gained or lost

- How their networks of influence are connected.

2. For each major stakeholder group, try to determine what their involvement might be: how much attention they will give you, how much support (or opposition) may be forthcoming, and what they may need or want from you.

3. Consider what they might be able to contribute to your effort. This table lists some questions you might want to find out about your stakeholders.

Who are the different groups?	Stakeholder groups can include local organizations, communities, businesses, interest groups, individuals, officials, and institutions, among others.
What influence and assets do they have?	Stakeholders have varied and multiple interests, skills, and resources. For example, they may be beneficiaries, gatekeepers, advisors, controllers, funders, legislators, subscribers, and employers.
What might they need or want from you?	They may have different needs and expectations of your department and its programs. Some groups might know little about you. Others may have inaccurate or skewed impressions of what you do. There may be some groups facing challenges or issues with which you could assist. Some groups might like to learn from you.
What can they contribute?	Stakeholders have a variety of resources which might be made available to you. These resources might include knowledge, skills, money, participation, materials, political support, advocacy, networking, and advice.
What more do you need to know?	Working effectively with stakeholders might require you to learn more about them, including their size, composition, history, personalities, leadership structure, rules, preferences, linkages, and positions on other issues, among other features.

An Example from an Internship Program

Here is an example of a relatively simple stakeholder analysis for an anthropology department's proposed internship program. For each major group of stakeholders, we can specify their involvement in the proposed program by using a matrix. The basic question is a simple one: Is there a 'market' for the internship program? Are stakeholders ready and willing to participate and support it?

If you do this sort of analysis at an early stage, you will avoid designing a program for which there is weak or nonexistent support.

- Columns list the principal stakeholders.
- Rows list five elements of marketing: need, product, price, communication system, and setup.

The matrix identifies five main groups of participants or stakeholders, and then asks five key questions:

- Why should people "buy into" this program?
- What is going to be required of them if they do buy in?
- What is it going to "cost" them?
- How do we reach them?
- How do we get things started?

	STAKEHOLDERS				
	Students	**Parents**	**Faculty/ Career Ctr.**	**Employers & Alumni**	**Financial Donors**
Need or problem Why are different target groups engaged in this program?	To improve student skills; to enable them to practice using anthropology; to make them more competitive on the job market	To give their children a competitive edge in the job market	To build enrollments; to acquire new knowledge; to derive professional satisfaction and recognition; to build and improve the program	To gain better trained and more competent entering professionals; to influence students to work for them	To gain prestige and recognition; to build institutional capacity; to increase public awareness of specific issues
Product How can these groups contribute to success?	Through time spent working in an organization, over an extended period of time	Through encouragement, and financial and emotional support	Through the establishment of networks and relationships with industry	Through internship programs linked to recruitment and training of entering professionals	Through funding, publicity and recognition
Price What will the stakeholders give in return?	Students must commit to the program and carry out all assigned tasks	Tuition dollars	Time spent on program design and management	Job placements and mentoring; logistic support	Financial and logistic support
Publicity How can we connect with the different groups?	Departmental and campus publicity; program requirements; advising	Recruitment brochures and information; Campus visiting days	Faculty information networks; special training and recruitment	Contacts with employers; network system for tracking	Marketing and networking with potential donors
Setup How can we get the program going?	Through faculty, industry contacts, and program coordinators	Through mailing and marketing	Workshops and training for faculty	Through site visits and networking	Through site visits, networking and funding proposals

6. Finding Clarity with Concept Maps

Riall W. Nolan

A concept map is a diagram or visual representation that illustrates relationships within a particular idea or concept. It is a useful way of helping groups formulate and express their ideas as they make plans. It encourages groups to think about what the term or concept means to them operationally, rather than relying on someone else's definition.

When setting out to do something—such as planning a new program or revising an existing one—it is important to be as specific as possible. A concept map takes a broad notion and breaks it into its constituent elements. Then, for each of the elements, concrete indicators of that element are listed.

Putting Concept Maps to Work

A concept map functions primarily as a springboard for discussion and further elaboration of the concept in question. In training groups, participants can be asked to create individual concept maps. The maps are compared and contrasted to form a fuller picture.

Concept maps may be a useful device in a department wondering how to modify the curriculum to improve student career readiness. Significant time will probably be spent defining, discussing, and debating the term "career ready," which is time well spent. The concept map will help department members track their progress in this discussion, and forge consensus on key points.

1. Give the idea, term, or concept a name. List it at the left of the diagram—or "map." Often, as discussion proceeds, this name changes.

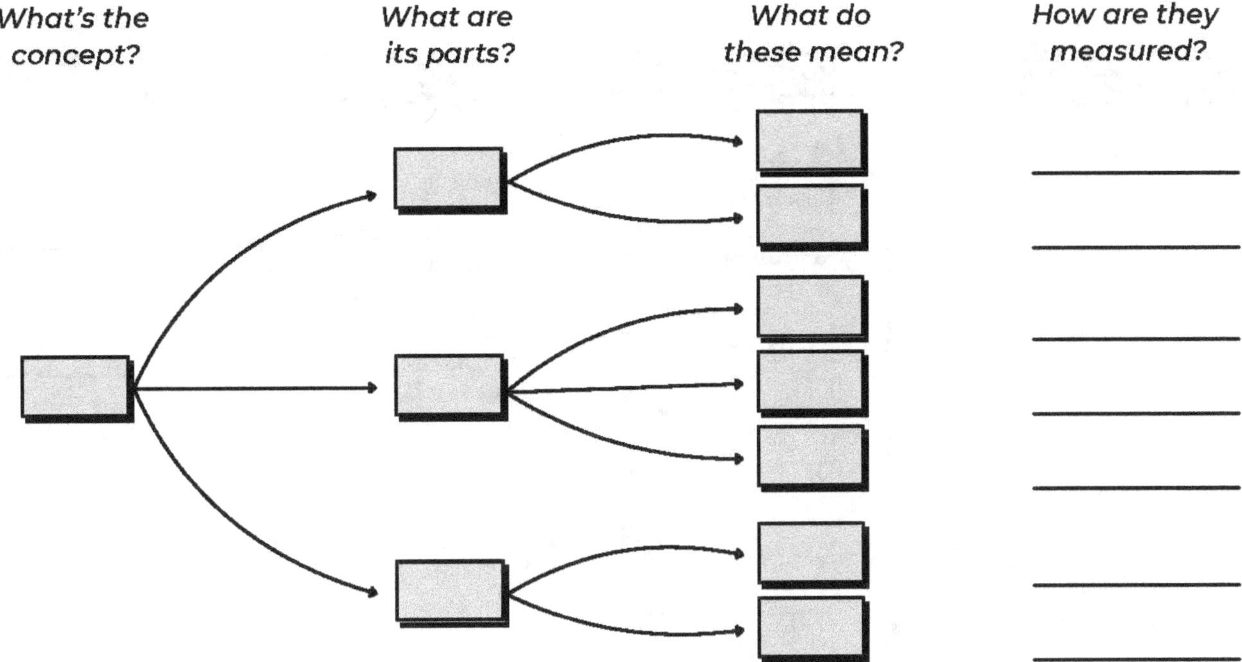

2. Specify the component parts of the concept. The second column lists some of these elements or attributes of the term. Few lists of attributes are exhaustive, but including the main ones will help focus the discussion and identify areas of agreement and consensus. These features can also change as the discussion proceeds.

3. Identify some of the details or behaviors associated with the attributes. The third column includes the most important ones, though not necessarily a complete list.

4. Develop a set of indicators. The final column lists measurable evidence or metrics which demonstrate whether the concept is in place.

An Example

This example of a concept map was developed for a local level non-governmental organization (NGO). You can see how this technique could be used in a department interested in making its curriculum more "career ready."

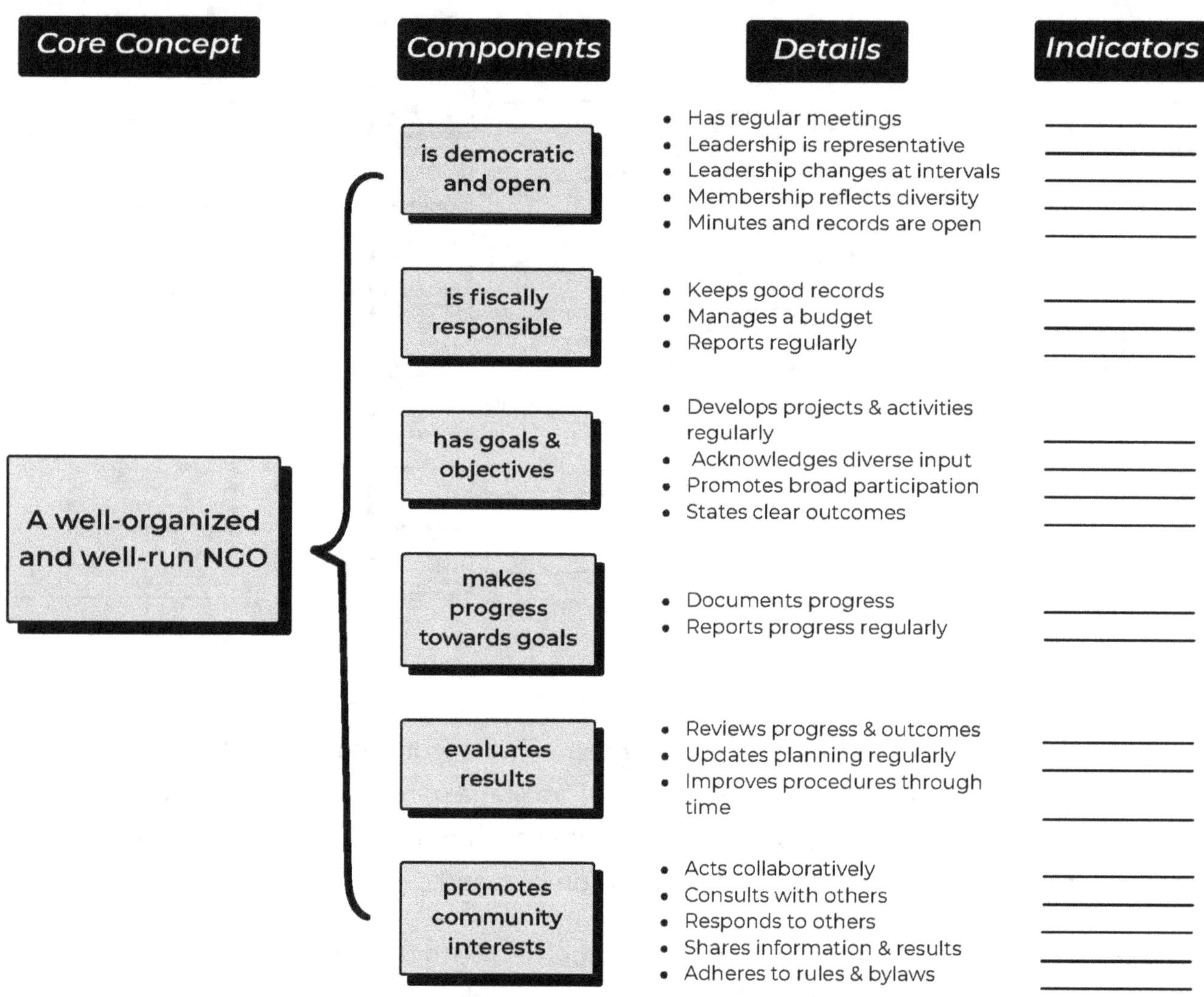

Using a concept map to help department members crystalize their thoughts, see what others are thinking, and examine the meaning of the terms and concepts generated, helps to focus the discussion and move it along. A concept map is particularly useful in helping people identify visible and measurable indicators of what they are talking about.

7. Establishing Common Ground on Career Readiness

Barry Dornfeld and Elizabeth K. Briody

Anthropology departments have operated as collections of researchers who teach students and participate in various service activities in their departments, institutions, and beyond. Academically-based anthropologists are largely autonomous, focused on their own research, courses, and responsibilities. Yet pressures from legislatures, university administrators, parents, and students have been rising for anthropology departments to prepare students for careers outside the gates of the academy. Noticeably, calls for career readiness abound, signaling new expectations for teaching and learning.

Meeting this challenge successfully requires a cultural change for anthropology departments from

- Instructor independence and insularity to greater cooperation, cohesion, and integration

- A single-minded emphasis on training students for academic careers to preparing them for a broader array of employment opportunities.

The focus of departments' work shifts to their visible customers—students—and their preparation for the future. If executed well, these changes would not only benefit students, but also departments through

- Student appreciation and recognizable achievements

- Expanded connections to organizations and communities

- Amended relationships with alumni

- Enhanced reputations.

This tool highlights two ways to explore and agree on a shared view of a departmental career readiness strategy. Two approaches are suggested.

1) Develop Your Departmental Vision and Mission

Meet with your colleagues to create vision and mission statements which use simple, clear language and are one sentence in length. These definitions, components, and examples provide guidance.

<table>
<tr><th>VISION</th><th>MISSION</th></tr>
<tr>
<td>

Definition:
An *aspirational declaration* focused on the future

Components:
- Offers direction, describing where the department is headed
- Represents the "big picture" of what departmental members hope to achieve together

Examples:
- **Google**: Provide access to the world's information in one click
- **Princeton Office of International Programs**: A community of collaborative learners who recognize our interdependence and work to advance justice and well-being
- **UNICEF**: A world where the rights of every child are upheld, enabling them to survive, thrive, and reach their full potential

</td>
<td>

Definition:
A statement identifying the broad *purpose* of what the department does, who the department serves, and how it provides value

Components:
- Specifies how the department will achieve its vision
- Guides decision making
- Steers external communications with stakeholders beyond the university

Examples:
- **Google**: To organize the world's information and make it universally accessible and useful
- **Princeton Office of International Programs**: To deliver ethical and collaborative community-based global learning experiences that foster critical thinking and work toward more just, inclusive, and sustainable communities
- **UNICEF**: To advocate for the protection of children's rights, to help meet their basic needs and to expand their opportunities to reach their full potential

</td>
</tr>
</table>

2) Agreeing on Your Departmental Strategy by Using a Relevant Framework

Developing vision and mission statements can be challenging because of the potential to get bogged down in abstractions. Another approach involves asking questions and making choices on your department's strategic impact, focus, and priorities. This approach could precede or follow the crafting of vision and mission statements. One helpful framework is the "strategy playbook"[1] which ACRN adapted from the original. The questions and the relationships across the six parts of the framework act as a choice cascade, with those at the top foundational and those at the bottom functioning to refine this foundation. These questions represent steps in the change process. Together they allow you to clarify, and ultimately operationalize, critical areas of departmental focus—in this case, career readiness.

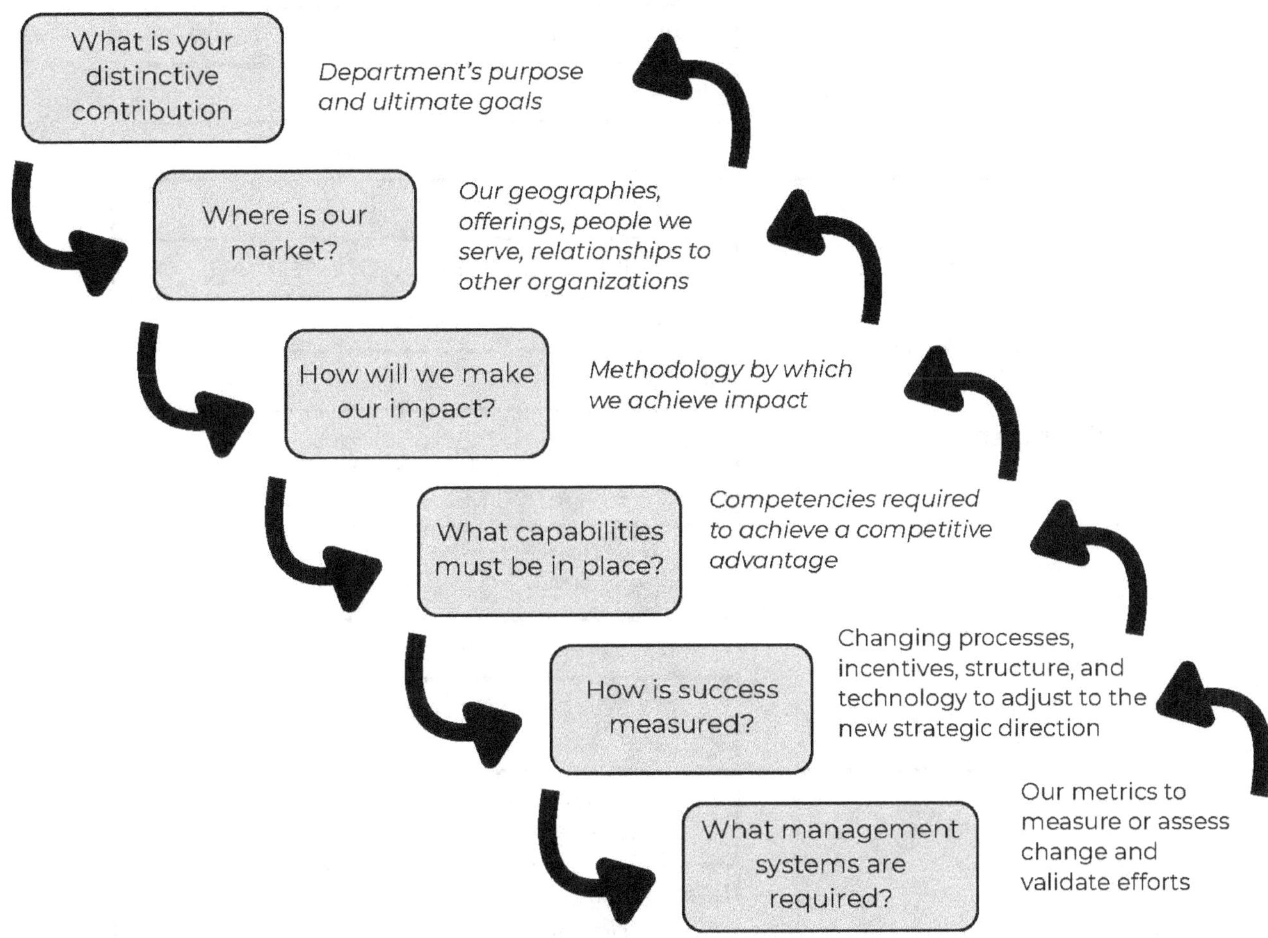

Explore this progression of departmental questions about career readiness and list your responses. Then, compare them with your colleagues' responses. The ACRN tool "Finding Clarity with Concept Maps" should be helpful as you conceptualize career readiness and what it entails.

The process for establishing common ground within your department is the same irrespective of approach. Departmental members convene to capture the spirit marking their collective identity and to shape a path forward. ACRN tools "Making Group Decisions through Discussion" and "Moving Forward with Consensus Decision Making" will be useful to you.

Departmental questions	Sample responses
Distinctive contribution?	Interdisciplinary strength
	Graduate career preparation
	Employability
Context and relationships?	Local client problem-solving opportunities
	Alumni access
	Tech business leader roundtable
Methodology?	Faculty-student ratio
	Mixed qualitative/quantitative methods
	Organizational fieldwork
Skills and abilities?	AI literacy
	Client engagement proficiency
	Effective internships
New processes and structures?	Required internship and internship preparation course
	Annual career panels
	Course syllabi name competencies that students acquire
Success?	Repeated mentions of career readiness (e.g., in meetings, on syllabi, on website)
	Steady progress toward meeting or exceeding metrics
	Stakeholder perceptions of improved career readiness

Reference

1. Martin, Roger, A.G. Lafley, and Jennifer Riel. 2013. "A Playbook for Strategy," *Rotman Magazine*, Winter.

8. Drafting Your Anthropology Department Roadmap

Carla Guerrón Montero, Jennifer Trivedi, Kedron Thomas, and Elizabeth K. Briody

A department roadmap is a visual plan that specifies program goals and the major activities tied to those goals. It illustrates the domains of knowledge, skill proficiencies, and hands-on experiences that students acquire as they complete the requirements for their degree. The roadmap is designed to portray what students learn as well as how to apply what they learn during fieldwork, internships, laboratory environments, and project work.

Rationale for a Roadmap

- Provide an overview and highlight distinctive features of your anthropology department for both internal university use (e.g., administrators, sister disciplines) and external use (e.g., prospective students, parents, organizational partners)

- Portray some department features sequentially, reinforcing individual building blocks as well as their cumulative effect

- Gauge progress toward a degree: what has been accomplished and what the future holds

"Our roadmap has been a game changer. It gives students a clear vision for how college pathways and opportunities connect to goals and aspirations beyond. It helps make the anthropology student experience more concrete, relatable, and compelling because the great value of our field as a source of human understanding is powerfully framed for career readiness and professional development."

- Peter Benson, Department Chair, University of Delaware

Roadmap Example with Selected Features

1. Core Training - Learn to Think Like an Anthropologist

- o   Contemporary theory
- o   Evolutionary principles

2. Domains of Knowledge - Explore Topics and Issues

- o   Cultural heritage management
- o   National vs. organizational cultures
- o   Migration and climate change

3. Skills - Develop Marketable Skills

- o   Project design and management
- o   Presentation and communication
- o   Content analysis
- o   Geographic Information System (GIS) and spatial analysis

4. Experiences - Apply Your Training

- o   Professionalization seminars and workshops
- o   Internships
- o   Field schools
- o   Networking events
- o   Client-based class projects

5. Graduate - Join Alumni Network

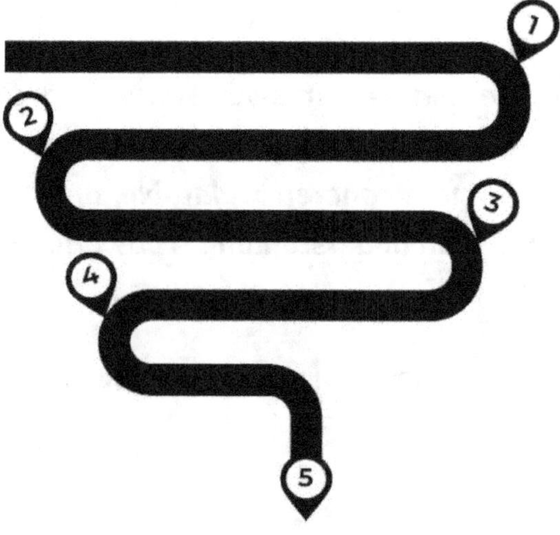

Process for Drafting Your Department Roadmap

- **Instructors** identify the 1) content, 2) skills, and 3) experiences associated with each of the courses they teach for *curriculum-related learning*

- **Staff and/or academic advisors** enumerate the co-curricular and extra-curricular activities (e.g., internships, workshops, service learning) for *departmental activities*

- **Analyst**

  - Compiles all department-sponsored learning and its frequency by course and in departmental programming

  - Identifies the key content, skills, and experiences of all department-sponsored learning

- **Department members** may review and offer input to validate the department analyst's draft

- **Designer**

  - Produces an initial roadmap design

  - Incorporates the key features (i.e., content, skills, experiences) into this design

- **Editor** adds supplementary text to clarify and/or explain the key features

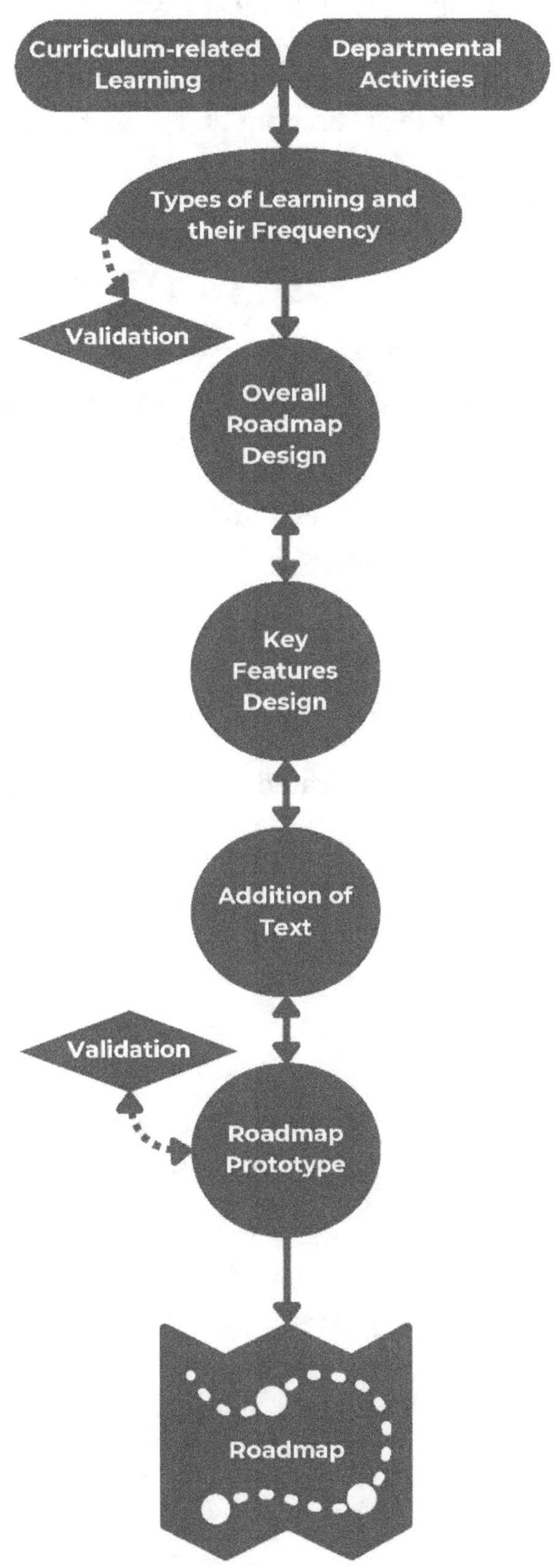

- **Department members** review the prototype roadmap to validate and offer suggestions for any changes

- **Prospective students and their parents** review the prototype as well; it is helpful to hear their reactions and listen to any comments they share

Value of the Roadmap

- Opens a window into what anthropology is, the competencies associated with it, and its application to problem solving in organizations and communities

- Represents a user-friendly visualization that invites interest and conversation, and is especially useful for distribution at public-facing events, to funders and senior administrators

- Helps publicize a discipline not known to promote itself

- Serves as a "living document" that can be modified over time

- Can be replicated on a smaller scale for anthropology minors, concentrations, and certificates

9. Putting Force Field Analysis to Work

Riall W. Nolan

Any situation in the everyday world is the result of a complex set of forces in the environment. Some of these forces push in one direction, and some in the opposite direction. The situation in front of you is the result of those forces.

It follows that if these forces were to change, or be changed, the outcome might very likely change. Force field analysis[1] is a well-recognized organizational development technique that can be used to help you understand these forces. And if you understand them, you may be able to change them.

The Value of Force Field Analysis

Force field analysis has been used for years in many different types of organizations. It can be very helpful to academic departments when defining or clarifying a goal, contemplating a change, or trying to understand the reasons why things are not changing. This process can provide department members with an appreciation of the various forces—positive as well as negative—that may be operating in a given situation and enable them to understand how these forces might be used to attain their objectives. Another virtue is its ability to help the department to develop a shared perspective and understanding regarding the issue or situation.

Process

1. Name or label the issue, situation, or problem.

The situation can refer to something already underway by your group or something the group might like to either attain or avoid in the future.

2. List the forces.

Driving or positive forces, as well as resisting or negative forces, will act on this issue, situation, or problem. The balance of these forces produces what you experience as the status quo.

3. Discuss and decide four linked questions.

- Of the driving and resisting forces listed, which ones can you influence in any way?
- Of the driving forces, which ones can you increase?
- Of the resisting forces, which ones can you weaken or eliminate?
- Which new forces can you introduce to affect the balance of forces?

An Example

Here is a fictitious example from an anthropology department which sought to increase the number of majors (Step 1). The faculty held <u>a brainstorming session</u> to determine ways to <u>increase the number of anthropology majors</u> while also recognizing the constraints they faced. This list of driving and resisting forces resulted (Step 2).

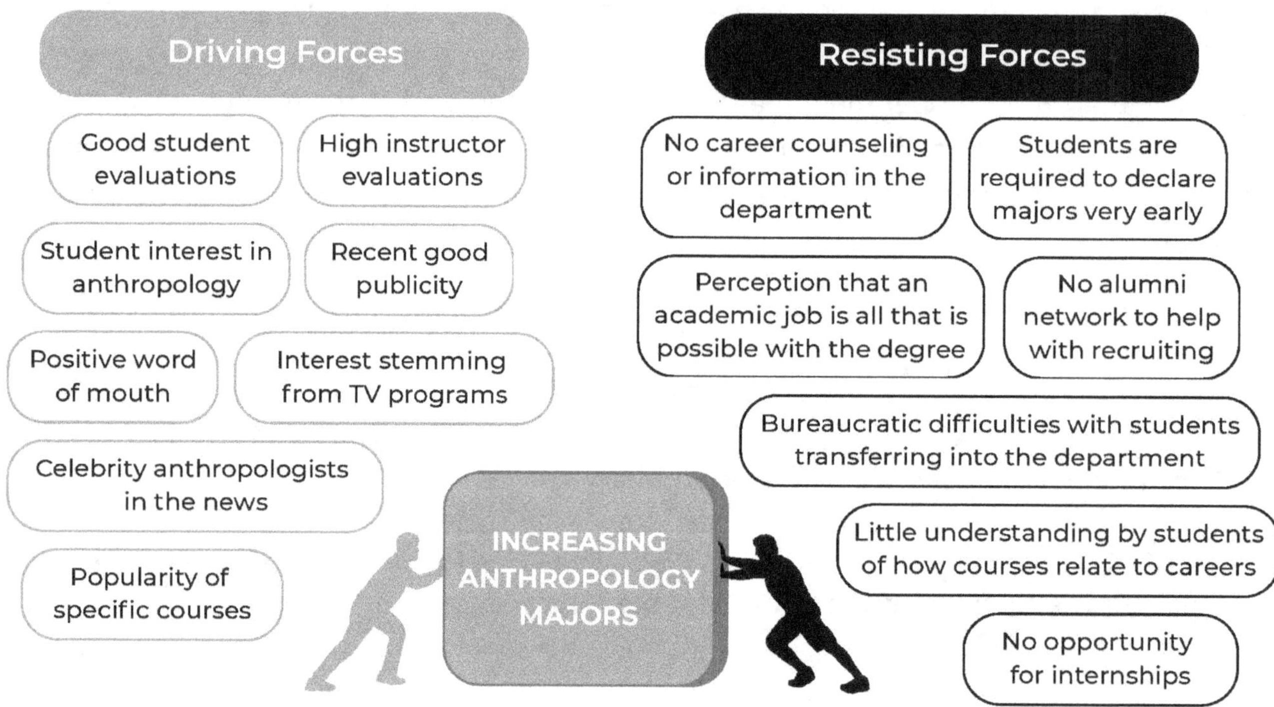

Then they focused on the four questions to problem solve around the driving and resisting forces (Step 3). The status quo can be altered by changing the strength and composition of the forces. It is probably easier to promote change by trying to weaken or eliminate some of the resisting forces than by attempting to strengthen the driving forces. It is also a good idea to focus on whether new driving forces can be brought to bear on the situation.

After discussion, the department decided to take the following actions:

- Begin attending recruitment fairs sponsored by their university

- Set up a booth at first-year orientation to feature anthropology

- Develop a schedule for visiting high schools in the area

- Reach out to Career Services on campus and work with them to help counsel students

- Set up a committee to develop an improved first-year introductory anthropology course focused on career opportunities (e.g., A Better ANTH 101)

- Set up a committee to look into an alumni outreach program

- Begin negotiations with the university to allow students more time to declare a major

This tool helps reveal the forces—positive and negative—that affect your program. It challenges you to work collaboratively to make your program as strong, robust, and healthy as possible.

Reference

1. Lewin, Kurt. 1943. "Defining the 'Field at a Given Time,'" *Psychological Review* 50(3): 292–310, May. Republished in *Resolving Social Conflicts & Field Theory in Social Science.* 1997. Washington, D.C.: American Psychological Association.

10. Using Brainstorming for Collaborative Problem Solving

Riall W. Nolan

Brainstorming is a technique used to stimulate group discussion, out-of-the-box thinking, and problem-solving, in a non-judgmental setting. It is useful for making lists, generating numerous ideas, and suggesting new approaches. It is particularly helpful for addressing new or unusual problems, situations where many people know some things, but no one knows everything. Brainstorming is also effective at the start of planning or problem-solving, as a way of ensuring that no valuable ideas get overlooked. Brainstorming sessions promote group collaboration, cohesion and a sense of common purpose, especially among people who may not work together all that often.

Assumptions

- Groups working together can generate a greater quantity of potentially useful ideas than can individuals working alone.
- Higher levels of creativity result by concentrating on the production of those ideas rather than on their ranking or evaluation.

Putting Brainstorming to Work

This technique can be applied in a variety of ways in a university context. For example, instructors may brainstorm how ethnographic methods used in organizational settings might be included in a field methods course. They may want to ensure that data analysis is taught in several courses but need to identify how those courses might accommodate such a change.

Brainstorming works best with five or more people. It requires a person to record and facilitate and some way to capture ideas. Large blackboards or whiteboards, or a large screen linked to a laptop, are ideal for capturing ideas. In a pinch, you can use Post-it notes. Whatever method you use, make sure that everyone can easily see all the ideas as they emerge.

Various AI platforms (e.g., ChatGPT) are also very good at generating large numbers of ideas; there is some evidence that they do a better job than humans. What they cannot do, of course, is create the shared creative experience of a group of people talking and working together.

Process

1. The purpose or objective for the session is set out and explained.

Everyone should agree on the purpose and its importance. State the problem clearly, but concisely, and explain why it is important to the group. You may want to state the problem or issue in the form of a question, such as *"How can we...?"*Other problem statements might take the form *"What if...?"* or *"I wish we could..."* Take time to seek agreement on the wording of this problem statement.

2. The rules for brainstorming are explained:

- No criticism or evaluation of ideas is allowed.
- Any idea is acceptable, even unusual ones; in fact, they may trigger other ideas.
- Quantity is more important than quality. Think of something to say, even if it is not up to your usual standard.
- Nobody 'owns' an idea. It is fine to add on to other ideas (hitchhiking) or to use another idea as the inspiration for your own (leapfrogging).
- All ideas are written down so that everyone can see them.

3. Generation of ideas begins.

In this phase, the goal is to produce as many suggestions as possible, without discussing or evaluating them. Ideas are written down as fast as they are generated.

- You can collect ideas randomly from the group, or in a more structured way, such as a "round robin" where the facilitator goes around the group allowing each person to contribute one idea at a time until no one has anything new to add.

- Other methods include having participants write out ideas on index cards or sticky notes, and then post them. Other participants can then add ideas to them.

4. Analysis of the ideas takes place.

Once a list is obtained, there is group discussion about the list of ideas which concentrates on:

- putting the ideas into categories or groups
- developing evaluative criteria.

New ideas may develop at this stage. They are noted and discussed.

You will need to spend some time discussing the criteria that are important to your group for identifying the "best" ideas. One very simple yet effective way of beginning this discussion is to have the group color code the various ideas. For example, using markers or colored dots, you can have participants mark ideas this way:

- Great ideas, very interesting
- Interesting ideas, but need work and/or clarification
- Intriguing, but something to think about more
- Not worth following up on

5. Planning for action.

Once the best ideas are identified, the group discusses how to implement them. Some of the better ideas can be acted upon at once; others will require planning and preparation. Some of the good ideas are relatively simple to implement while others are complex and difficult.

Using brainstorming effectively requires group discipline and patience. It also requires a skilled facilitator who can nudge the group back on track if necessary. Finally, it works best with relatively well-defined problems, to which the solutions or approaches are not immediately clear.

Your group can explore other techniques for creative problem solving in addition to brainstorming (such as force-field analysis). You might also consider using an AI platform to help you generate ideas. But there is no doubt that with a good facilitator, a diverse and engaged group of participants, and a clear objective or problem statement, brainstorming can be a valuable tool for problem solving, co-creation, and the promotion of positive group dynamics.

Advantages and Disadvantages of Brainstorming

ADVANTAGES

- Fast and exciting
- Best when the group already knows and likes each other
- Lack of criticism usually stimulates creative imagination
- Visual as participants can see the ideas as they emerge
- Generates novel suggestions
- Promotes cross-fertilization
- Relatively unstructured, may lead to 'breakthroughs'
- Seeing ideas produces 'snow-balling' of other ideas
- Most effective when problem is simple and specific

DISADVANTAGES

- Problems need to be small and precisely defined to be managed
- Can be expensive and time-consuming to bring participants together
- Process may degenerate into mere 'fun'
- Does not work well with timid people
- Does not work well with groups which are suspicious of each other
- Does not always work in groups with marked status differences
- May not work well with sensitive or highly controversial topics
- May not generate anything useful
- Strong individuals may dominate the group
- May not work with new members
- Discussion may become misdirected

11. Making Group Decisions through Discussion

Riall W. Nolan

Most university instructors are used to making straightforward decisions in their work. The choices present themselves simply and clearly such as: *Should I assign this reading or that one?* Depending on their role and institution, instructors often have the ability to make decisions individually and unilaterally—that is, by themselves, to suit themselves.

However, some decisions need to be made by groups, often under conditions of uncertainty and ambiguity. In these decisions, the difference between "right" and "wrong" answers is either not apparent, or other people's wishes have to be considered. Often, we will not know for some time whether we have made wise choices. In these situations, many decisions have outcomes affecting not only ourselves and our department, but others including students.

Therefore, it is helpful to look briefly at some aspects of group decision making.

Components of Successful Discussions

A variety of elements contribute to effective group meetings. Having a good facilitator is key. In addition, a successful meeting will depend on:

- **Facts as well as Opinions:** Some members know more than others; everyone knows something, but no one is likely to know everything. Distinguishing fact from opinion is crucial.

- **Knowledge:** Knowledge refers to how an assemblage of facts are put together. Some group members may be better than others at "connecting the dots." Others may have detailed knowledge about the context surrounding the various facts.

- **Experience and Judgment:** Those possessing first-hand experience with the issues under discussion will be able to provide more insight.

- **Collegiality:** A willingness to work well with one another, listen to and respect differing views, and seek common solutions are essential. Skill in co-thinking and co-creating will be valuable.

Big and Little Decisions

You should also differentiate between big, important decisions and ones that are smaller and less important. Big decisions need to be made carefully and typically incorporate these features:

- **Size or Length of Commitment:** How much in the way of resources (e.g., time, energy, money) is involved? How long is the period of commitment? A decision that costs more in these terms may be one which requires more care.

- **Flexibility:** Is this decision irrevocable? Can it be reversed or only modified?

- **Uncertainty:** To what extent are you confident in your logic, facts, and assumptions? If you decide to do something, are you sure you will be able to do it? Are you sure that if you do it, you will get the expected results? Uncertain conditions or outcomes may require more thought, especially when views are unclear or divided.

- **Quantifiability of Variables:** Can the various factors involved be measured easily or are they highly subjective?

- **Outcomes:** What are the likely human, financial, and organizational impacts? Are there negative or dangerous consequences?

- **Periodicity:** How often does this decision have to get made? If it recurs in the same form fairly frequently, it is probably worth investing the time to make the "right" decision once, to avoid having to "reinvent the wheel" in the future.

A Discussion Framework

Meetings called to make decisions, plan new activities, or solve problems need careful facilitation and an overt awareness of process if they are to be successful. This framework[1] is useful for meeting discussions of this kind.

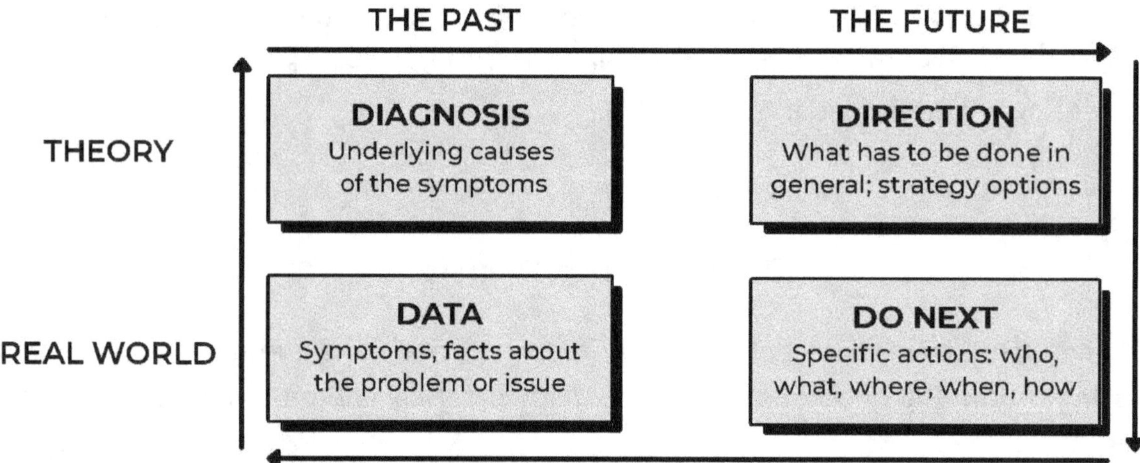

Typically, discussion moves freely back and forth between "the real world" of facts and the world of theory, and between the past (i.e., what has happened and why) and the future (i.e., what should be done and how). Successful meetings are ones which do not neglect any of these four quadrants. A good facilitator can make sure that the group discussion covers all four quadrants.

Considerations

Decision-making meetings will need to consider the following:

- **Ripeness:** Sometimes, it is clearly time to make a decision and other times, it is clearly *not* the time for a decision. Being able to distinguish one situation from the other is essential.

- **Scope:** What sort of response is required from your group: a solution, suggestion, several suggestions, an opinion? Before you begin your discussion, decide what your end goal is.

- **Solution requirements (must-haves):** If you need a solution, are there specific characteristics of that solution (e.g., cost, speed, complexity) which must be either present or absent?

- **Theory before practice:** Coming up with a decision that "fits" *before* looking at how to make that decision work is a basic rule of <u>brainstorming</u> but should be applied in many other situations. Often, the best decisions are made in an atmosphere of unfettered creativity, where objections are saved for later, after a series of possible solutions have emerged.

- **Action and feedback:** A decision will do you no good if nothing happens. Make sure that the decision is actionable, and that someone is assigned to implement it. Keep track of the outcome of any decision that you implement. Make sure that you have, or can get, the information necessary to assess the results.

- **Documentation:** Ensure that you remember what you decided and why you did it that way. Keep a record for future reference.

Reference

1. Fisher, Roger and Alan Sharp. 1998. *Getting It Done: How to Lead When You're Not in Charge.* New York, NY: Harper Business, p. 79.

12. Moving Forward with Consensus Decision Making

Riall W. Nolan

The consensus method is a collective decision-making process. The essence of consensus is **agreement**: all members of the group must agree with the decision(s). Consensus decision making does not mean that the decision is the ideal or optimal one for each group member; merely that they "can live with" the decision. Therefore, consensus implies a degree of compromise between what is preferred ideally and what is acceptable pragmatically. It requires active support of the decision.

Decisions are not always made by consensus. Many decisions which affect the workplace are made unilaterally, by committee, or by others further up the hierarchy. And when we make decisions as a group, we often default to the "majority rule" method which works fairly well most of the time. However, majority-rule votes can often ignore a sizeable minority which may cause problems later. Other solutions to a problem such as splitting the group, leadership-driven decision making, and bargaining are not acceptable under consensus decision making.

Putting Consensus Decision Making to Work

Consensus can be useful in a variety of situations. When the problem affects everyone or where the solutions available are going to impact everyone, consensus may be required. Occasionally, single individuals may be able to block action and so consensus must be sought. In other cases, it may be necessary for the group to present a united front, and to defend their decision strongly against outside opposition or pressure. Here again, consensus may be the best decision-making option.

In an academic setting, decisions requiring consensus might include the selection of a new department chair, the hiring of a new faculty member, or a substantial change in the curriculum. In these and similar cases, you may want to seek consensus rather than a show-of-hands vote.

Guidelines for the Group

- Define the problem in terms which are simple and acceptable to all group members.

- Use a facilitator, particularly if the group is large in size and if the decision is important.

- Encourage each other to share ideas and pool information before coming to a decision. Talk about interests, expectations, or basic needs and wants.

- Avoid discussing issues in terms of positions or bargaining stances. Distinguish instead between someone's stated position on an issue and their underlying interest or concern.[1] Use these common concerns or interests as a base for generating suggestions acceptable to all.

- Break large problems down into smaller ones if deadlocks arise.

- Within a large group, form temporary 'sub-committees' if a few individuals seem unable to resolve differences. Send them away for private discussions, and re-form when differences have been ironed out.

- Stress throughout that individuals need only reach agreement on minimally acceptable solutions, not optimum ones.

- Avoid conflict-reducing techniques such as majority rule, averaging, trading, or bargaining to reach your decisions.

- Do not 'reward' people for conceding. View differences of opinion as a help rather than a hindrance in decision making. Seek out those differences of opinion and incorporate them into the discussion. The more distinctive viewpoints you discuss, the more alternatives you will generate.

Guidelines for Individual Participants

It is easier to reach consensus if you avoid arguing for your own individual judgments. Present your position clearly, but listen to others' reactions and consider them carefully before pressing your point. Approach the task on the basis of logic. Try not to think in win-lose terms, but rather in terms of the next-most-acceptable alternative.

On the other hand, do not change your mind simply to avoid conflict and reach agreement. Yield only to positions that seem to be objectively and logically sound. Support only solutions with which you are able to agree at least somewhat.

Advantages and Disadvantages of Consensus Decision Making

ADVANTAGES

- Group members do not have to be particularly skilled
- The process often brings people together who do not normally interact much
- Data is shared among the entire group
- The talents of everyone are used
- The group-building ambiance that results can be carried over into other situations
- Widely different skills and experiences can be fit together
- Group members usually learn new and useful information about one another that improves future interactions
- A high degree of commitment to the decision usually results

DISADVANTAGES

- Everyone must agree on the definition of the problem
- One or two intransigent members can block the group
- The group's data pool may be insufficient
- This process may not work well with many members
- It is time consuming and, in some cases, inefficient
- A very high degree of commitment by members is required
- The group may be influenced by persuasive or dominant members
- Individual differences may be too great to allow for solutions which encompass them
- The discussion process may uncover problems rather than solving them

Reference

1. Fisher, Roger, William Ury and Bruce Patton. (2011) *Getting to Yes: Negotiating Agreement Without Giving In*. 3rd ed. New York, NY: Penguin.

13. Improving Anthropology's Visibility on Campus

Megan O'Brien-Rene

Many anthropology departments are struggling to attract and retain students. ACRN's tool <u>Boosting Anthropology Enrollments</u> offers several strategies for anthropology departments at risk of shrinking, shuttering, or being combined. Another effective strategy involves tapping into the potential of your own students and recent graduates.

This tool builds on the results of five focus groups involving 20 participants from both North America and abroad. It captures the emic perspective of anthropology undergraduates and graduate students as well as recent graduates. Key focus group questions included:

- What attracted you to anthropology?

- Think back to any department events you have attended. What made them stand out or feel successful?

- If you were the head of an anthropology department, what would you do differently to make the field more appealing, accessible, and easier to envision career paths?

By learning directly from the experiences and ideas of the focus group participants, the tool offers departments practical initiatives to sponsor and support.

Student and recent graduate ideas were grouped into eight initiatives designed to heighten anthropology's awareness on campus, lead to a rise in enrollment and majors, and enhance understanding of anthropology's relevance and application in the world. These initiatives represent actions department members can take to improve visibility on campus.

1. Facilitating Early Exposure and Outreach: Learning about anthropology prior to entering college is crucial to spreading awareness and understanding of anthropology's value and relevance, as well as building interest and increasing anthropology enrollment and majors.

- Partner with high schools to a) introduce anthropology earlier in students' educational journey, and b) increase the number of first-year students declaring anthropology as their major.

- Promote anthropology during college orientations to ensure incoming students are aware of the discipline of anthropology.

- Seek to include introductory courses as part of General Education requirements to ensure all students, regardless of major, are exposed to anthropology. And, to see a surge in interest, consider this ACRN tool: <u>A Better ANTH 101</u>.

2. Improving Marketing and Recruiting: Anthropology could compete effectively with popular majors on campus with ongoing, targeted, and visible strategies demonstrating that it can be applied across any profession.

- Distribute flyers customized for specific majors/interests to demonstrate anthropology's relevance in practical ways:

    o "How Anthropology Can Enhance Your Major" (e.g., pre-med, pre-law, engineering, business)

    o "5 Reasons Psychology Majors Should Study Anthropology"

    o "How Cultural Anthropology Makes You a Better Traveler."

- Engage with and use social media/event apps to connect the department with a wider audience and normalize anthropology as a visible, exciting field.

- Utilize QR codes to connect students instantly to department initiatives.

- Provide incentives (e.g., snacks, extra credit, raffle prizes) to attend events to boost turnout, start conversations, and create "buzz."

- Utilize swag as an effective, low-cost way to raise awareness and spark conversation in a "no pressure" and "casual" environment and where no prior knowledge of anthropology is needed for getting involved.

- Utilize new forms of marketing (e.g., guerrilla marketing) and zines (i.e., creative magazines) to grab student attention and keep marketing strategies relevant.

- Create course titles that peak student interest in anthropology (e.g., <u>Promoting Courses with a Dash of Pop Culture</u>).

- Design and disseminate an anthropology newsletter that appeals to a variety of disciplines on campus.

3. Ensuring Equity, Access, and Representation: Efforts are needed to bridge the gap with student communities that are unaware of anthropology.

- Plan specific outreach to student populations that may have limited exposure to the value and relevance of non-traditional career paths (e.g., anthropology with health sciences).

- Tailor campaigns to highlight students who want to empower underserved communities, thereby making a difference in the world. The ability to understand diverse perspectives positions these students to explore their interests and passions as subject matter experts and advocates (e.g., working with Tribes on cultural resource management, immigration policy, differences in worker management perspectives, the complexity of the Black Lives Matter Movement).

4. Strengthening Events and Clubs: Events and clubs are essential to improving anthropology's visibility because they encourage student interaction beyond their courses. ("Clubs" in this context refers to interest-based rather than disciplinary-based groups.) However, because student have priorities (e.g., their studies, jobs, responsibilities), these activities need to be worth their limited free time.

- Characteristics of Successful Events and Clubs:

  o Anthropology departments are directly involved in the events and clubs.

  o The events and clubs result in a high frequency of engaging experiences as well as increased visibility for anthropology.

  o Ongoing recruitment of new club members occurs, mindful of taking campus diversity into account.

  o A "no pressure" atmosphere is evident: prior knowledge about anthropology is not required so that students with varying interests from any discipline are welcomed.

- o Holding live streams/recording programs ensure that events are available to online/hybrid students.

  - o Providing incentives for students to attend (e.g., bringing along friends) is incorporated into the planning.

  - o When guest speakers are highlighted, career path and subfield diversity are taken into consideration.

- Job Search and Job Skills Events

  - o Students learn to present on anthropology's role in the community and state and then deliver what they have learned in at least one local organization.

  - o A student-led, event-planning short course offers practical experience, leadership skills, and departmental engagement.

  - o <u>Career fairs</u> and expos can highlight organizations and companies employing anthropologists.

  - o Career/<u>resume</u> workshops are organized which are appropriate to a variety of anthropology careers.

  - o <u>Job application</u> workshops are designed to improve student self-confidence during the application process.

- Examples of Creative and Engaging Events

  - o Skill development (e.g., shovel scraping and sieving, drawing/painting artifacts)

  - o Contests (e.g., trivia nights, game nights)

  - o Workshops (e.g., zines) in collaboration with a local business raffle

  - o Social events (e.g., end-of-semester potluck, international culture nights, DJ nights)

5. Emphasizing Career Pathways: Students need help learning about anthropology's versatility and practical applications.

- Offer courses with readings[1] based on real-world impact to highlight anthropology's emphasis on problem solving and implementation.

- Clearly label and promote content that uses anthropological methods so that audiences learn to recognize anthropology's distinctive features.

- Provide students with information.

    - Introduce students to ACRN's Exploring Possible Careers or the National Association for the Practice of Anthropology's sNAPAshots.

    - Hold networking opportunities with alumni for students to start building their networks pertaining to possible career paths.

    - Offer specialty training for the job hunt and beyond (e.g., informational interviews, elevator pitch, Excel, Geographic Information System).

- Anthropology departments need to incorporate work and skill experiences into their courses.

    - Incorporate client-based class projects and service learning in local organizations and communities.

    - Establish internships as a program requirement.

    - Assign project outcomes as part of coursework (e.g., op-ed article, blogpost, student video).

    - Explore local field school opportunities to increase attendance and reduce costs.

    - Encourage senior thesis and capstone projects that are anthropologically rich, publication worthy, and/or organizationally relevant for the domains students plan to pursue after graduation.

    - Consider professor-supervised research with publication as a goal for high-GPA juniors.

6. Teaching Students to Explain Anthropology's Usefulness So They Can Serve as Ambassadors: Students are often uncomfortable talking about their major because they do not know how to explain anthropology, how it applies to the real-world, or the types of jobs for which they might be qualified.

- Provide students with case examples of how anthropology can be useful in a variety of careers and project work[2].

- Strengthen student awareness of and confidence in their <u>anthropological skills</u> so they are conversant in discussing how they would approach solving a problem.

- Provide students with unique and relatable ways to <u>explain anthropology to others</u> using examples:

    o Being an anthropologist is like having a tool belt where you pick the appropriate tools to apply—given the problem or research question.

    o A graph shows the relationship between two variables. Anthropologists dig deeper to explain the emerging patterns and correlations.

    o The versatility of anthropology is like a DJ whose knowledge of theory and skills mix and match based on the project in which they are engaged.

- Encourage students to be anthropology ambassadors by promoting their major to peers who express curiosity and interest in it.

- Facilitate annual discussions/surveys to ask anthropology students how the department might improve.

7. Facilitating Interdepartmental Collaboration: Bridging the gap between anthropology and other disciplines can demonstrate the benefit to all fields.

- Host events with other departments to show overlapping themes and real-world applications (e.g., anthropology and environmental studies)

- Invite professors trained in anthropology but working in other departments/schools of the university to deliver a guest lecture or participate on a career panel highlighting the connections between anthropology and their area of work.

- Encourage professors in other departments to suggest anthropology as a minor or elective to a) help their students in their major, and b) build an academic culture that values anthropology's cross-disciplinary strengths.

- Facilitate interdepartmental student collaboration projects to allow students the opportunity to apply their anthropological skills (e.g., ethnography and film).

- Hold an interdisciplinary research week for students to share how anthropology combines well with other disciplines.

8. Encouraging Department-Alumni Relationships: Providing guidance in navigating the transition from academia to the job search increases students' knowledge base and confidence. <u>Potential activities with alumni</u> can support this initiative.

- Ask alumni guest speakers to share their career paths and networking tips.

- Hold alumni-student networking events to help students feel more comfortable and confident about their future career options.

- Design student projects to a) develop alumni profiles for your department website or b) produce a documentary on alumni careers. These projects highlight diverse career paths and offer students insight into what their future careers might be.

- Create an online platform for graduating anthropology students to share their research and job search strategies so that they serve as a source of inspiration for new majors.

References

1. Nolan, Riall W. 2026. *Using Anthropology in the World: A Guide to Becoming an Anthropologist Practitioner*. 2 ed. New York, NY: Taylor & Francis; Artz, Matt and Lora Koycheva, eds. 2025. *EmTech Anthropology: Careers at the Frontier*. New York, NY: Taylor & Francis.

2. Redding, Terry M. and Charles C. Cheney, eds. 2022. *Profiles of Anthropological Praxis: An International Casebook*. New York, NY: Berghahn; Wulff, Robert M. and Shirley J. Fiske, eds. 1987. *Anthropological Praxis: Translating Knowledge into Action*. Boulder, CO: Westview Press.

14. Building Department-Alumni Connections

Elizabeth K. Briody

Most anthropology programs do not have practices in place to help them maintain connections with their graduates. Alumni are often an untapped resource willing to assist students from their alma mater with career advice and preparation, and networking.

How does your program benefit?

- Dedicated pool of potential speakers and workshop presenters
- Source of class projects with an alum's organization as client
- Professional input on program features
- Pipeline to internships and job opportunities
- Co-teaching or teaching a course

How do your students benefit?

- Learning to form professional relationships
- Workplace knowledge and skill acquisition
- Advising on professionalization skills, internships, and job search

How do your alumni benefit?

- Ability to "pay it forward" to the next generation
- Access to campus resources (e.g., meeting with faculty, library electronic access)
- Continued connection to the discipline, academia, and other alumni
- Exposure to current student ideas and input
- Expansion of their networks with the next-generation workforce
- Pool of applicants for internships and jobs

What are strategies for staying in touch?

Many strategies work well in alumni outreach and in building long-term relationships with them. (Such strategies also demonstrate alumni value and departmental career preparation efforts to administrators.) While in-person may be preferred, much programming can be virtual, so start experimenting:

- **<u>Launch a LinkedIn Group</u>** of alumni that can be accessed by both instructors and students to network and build community.

- **Ask an Alum to be a Speaker or Workshop Presenter** for a particular course or the anthropology program as a whole.

- **Create an <u>Alumni Advisory Board</u>** that meets with departmental leaders on a recurring basis to discuss emergent career fields, student preparation for a changing workplace, and relevant skills, methods, and experiences among new hires—all of which can help shape your anthropology program.

- **Welcome Alums Back to Campus** annually for a day of scheduled programming and/or informal conversations.

- **Convene an Alumni Panel** mid-semester that focuses on career preparation, skill development, and careers highlighting anthropology.

- **Seek Alumni Advice** on a range of topics such as case studies of ethical workplace dilemmas, teaching methods relevant in organizational research, and building an internship program.

- **Invite Alumni to <u>Campus Career Fairs</u>** where they can represent their organizations, advertise for open positions, and speak with students.

- **Ask Alumni to Serve as Judges** for best capstone portfolios; annual departmental poster contest based on local organizational or community research; or short podcasts of an "amazing anthropologist" working in industry, non-profits, or government.

15. Launching and Sustaining a Community Advisory Board

Keri Vacanti Brondo and Elizabeth K. Briody

Anthropology departments have opportunities to reach out into the communities around them for knowledge and information, advice, and funding—including internships and job pipelines. Establishing a Community Advisory Board can enhance anthropology coursework and programming for students while streamlining the connection between the university and the workforce.

"We have benefited tremendously from our Board: constructive feedback on significant local issues, guidance on our curriculum, identification of specific skills to be competitive in the job market, advice on how they navigated their careers, internship opportunities at their workplaces, community-based research experience in our classes, help with writing our Department mission, vision, and value statements, and so much more."

- Keri Vacanti Brondo, former Associate Dean and Department Chair, University of Memphis, Memphis, TN; currently Lambros Comitas Chair of Anthropology, Teachers College, Columbia University, New York, NY

Board's Role

- Offer working world perspectives on organizational challenges, changing technology, current trends, and expectations for new hires

- Provide general input on curriculum updates

- Participate in department career readiness initiatives (e.g., training, networking events, speaker series)

- Advise and mentor selected students

- Help bridge the flow of people from the department to local organizations:

    o Supervise internships and practica which frequently lead to employment
    o Facilitate problem solving efforts and consulting arrangements
    o Collaborate as research partners with faculty

- Help with departmental fundraising efforts

- Recruit new community partners as Board members

Possible Board Members

- Local organizational leaders (e.g., businesspeople, nonprofit managers, municipal leaders)

- Alumni

- Anthropologists working in industry, nonprofits, and government

Department Members Working with the Board

- Faculty

- Staff

Department's Role

- Identify and invite between five to ten individuals to serve on the Board for two to three years on a staggered rotation

- Convene and coordinate Board meetings at least twice annually for faculty and staff with Board members

- Orient the Board to the department, presenting updates on department members and activities related to Board interests

- Coordinate activities (e.g., panels, networking events, presentations) involving students and Board members

- Enable Board members to deliver class lectures, co-teach, and teach courses

- Involve university staff (e.g., career planning, marketing) in Board activities, as appropriate

- Publicly recognize and thank Board members for their contributions

Effective Board Practices

- Designate one department member to be the Co-Chair and primary contact person for all Board business

- Invite one Board member to serve as Co-Chair and collaborate with the department's Co-Chair on Board business

- Survey Board members to gather their insights on what specific contribution they would like to offer

- Plan and carry out Board meetings

  - Poll Board and department members for a convenient day and time for Board meetings; when possible, keep to that day and time during the academic year
  - Prepare an agenda for each meeting and send it out in advance
  - Establish meeting expectations:
    - Follow the agenda
    - Use a scribe or record the meeting
    - Take turns speaking
    - Seek specific Board member actions to support the department
    - Make decisions
    - End meetings promptly
  - Make use of the Chat function when Board meetings are conducted virtually
  - Send out meeting minutes (i.e., notes), including follow-up tasks, as well as the Chat after the Board meeting has ended

- Form small working groups of department and Board members to plan upcoming activities, as appropriate

- Foster strong and effective relationships between department and Board members

  - Thank Board members for their participation during each meeting

- o Invite Board members to at least two social events each year (e.g., dinner, party)
  - o Seek regular feedback from Board members on their involvement, implementing change as appropriate
  - o Publicly recognize the efforts of outstanding Board members

Benefits for the Department

- Acquire fresh outsider perspectives on department coursework and programming

- Learn about new external forces and trends shaping area organizations

- Gain exposure to the pragmatics of organizational functioning, decision making, and planned change

- Extend professional networks into area businesses, nonprofits, and local governmental agencies

- Get advice on curriculum, training, professionalization skills, and job search processes

- Obtain programming for department members in the form of presentations, workshops, panels, and social events, among others

- Enable class lectures and co-teaching by Board members, as appropriate

- Establish job shadowing, internship, fundraising, and research and consulting project opportunities, as well as job pipelines

- Extend student mentoring beyond the university to community partners

Benefits for Board Members

- Create and build their university connections

- Use their positions to help bridge the flow of people from university to local organizations

- Train and hire new talent from the university to advance their organizations and missions

- Get assistance from faculty and students in the form of class projects and consulting on thorny organizational issues

- Gain alternative perspectives on issues of the day from the diversity of thought and practices in the university

- Gain satisfaction from offering their ideas, suggestions, and opportunities to others, "paying it forward" to the next generation

16. Boosting Anthropology Enrollments

Zahra Malik, JiangJiang (JJ) Wu, Jonathan Geyer, Irene Greene, and Riall W. Nolan

Student enrollments are an important metric for measuring the health of a department. Anthropology enrollments and number of declared majors are decreasing, putting a number of anthropology departments at risk of shrinking, shuttering, or being combined with other departments. A variety of strategies are outlined in this tool to boost the number of students in your programs. Successful implementation requires planning, consensus, and collaboration over a period of several years as well as the institutionalization of arrangements so that gains do not disappear.

Why are anthropology enrollments falling?

- Negative press about anthropology and outdated public perception

- Pressure from legislators, administrators and parents for employability and greater attention to career readiness

- Growing emphasis on career readiness works against those anthropology departments that cannot clearly demonstrate their workforce relevance

- Overall reduction in General Education requirements

- Opportunities to take introductory college courses through less expensive community colleges, online, or in high school

- Competition from diversity-oriented courses (e.g., gender studies, African American studies)

- Demographic shift leading to fewer people enrolling in college overall

Why boost anthropology enrollments?

- Higher enrollments in introductory classes will eventually mean more majors, thereby increasing:

    - demand for courses and instructors
    - increased student exposure to anthropological thinking
    - opportunities for students to learn from each other

- More majors mean more anthropology graduates whose departments have adapted, reducing the possibility of cuts, downsizing, or closure

- More graduates from career ready programs mean more and better jobs and greater awareness of anthropology's relevance and value across workplaces

Starting a Departmental Enrollment Initiative

Do we really need to take on this enrollment initiative?

- Anthropology BAs have dropped 23% between 2011-23 (U.S. Dept. of Education, IPEDS, https://nces.ed.gov/ipeds/)

- This decline has reduced the pool of graduate students and the number of new professors and staff hired

What does a departmental enrollment initiative entail?

It is a comprehensive, department-wide approach involving instructors, staff, and students with the goal of being student focused.

What are the benefits of a departmental enrollment initiative?

- Higher enrollment, with an impact on more students

- Strengthened department collaboration, resulting in a more interactive and vibrant community

- Greater student-instructor interaction with benefits to both

- Improved awareness and respect for the department within the university, enhancing opportunities for additional funding and research partnerships

- Opportunity for the department to grow in number of instructors and staff

What enrollment metrics can help track the initiative's progress?

- Proportion of instructors, staff, and students engaged in the effort

- Number of inquiries about the program

- Number of students in introductory courses

- Number of majors and minors

Strategies for Implementation

To build enrollments, your plan needs to be strategic, collective, and long term. The following suggested strategies fall into three broad categories:

1. Curriculum Changes

2. Relationship Building

3. Marketing and Public Outreach

You and your colleagues know your situation the best, so select what works for your department. For as many of these suggestions as possible, emphasize the application and career aspects.

1. Curriculum Changes

Existing Course Updates - None of these options requires new course development. In a few cases, minor adjustments or rebranding are involved. In other cases, you may want to re-think course prerequisites to encourage greater enrollment.

- Reclassify courses so they fit with university core requirements

- Tweak introductory courses so that they fit the General Education or core requirements

- Invigorate introductory courses to include a focus on issues of the day, project work, and careers, see ACRN's A Better ANTH 101 tool

- Rewrite course titles and descriptions to emphasize contemporary issues (e.g., Anthropology of Social Media, Ghost Stories across Cultures)

- Cross-list more courses with other departments to introduce more students to anthropology

- Collaborate with the Honors College to make entry into anthropology courses easier

- Provide "dual-enrollment options" through which high school students can earn college credit

- Incorporate client-based class projects into several existing courses so that students gain project experience, learn to work and problem solve as team members, and develop new skills

- Create an option for students to shadow local anthropologists during the workday

- Indicate which career ready skills will be introduced and practiced by course

- Specify the methods that students will be taught by course

- Identify the work-related experiences (e.g., client projects, fieldwork, internships) students will have by course

- Use ACRN's Career Ready Curriculum to generate ideas for new modules in your courses and expand student knowledge of anthropological practice

- Have instructors teach in some of the interdisciplinary topics courses (i.e. Diversity, Animal Behavior, Nutrition)

New Course Offerings - Some of these ideas will attract new students but not necessarily new majors. Others are designed to influence first-year students and persuade them to declare anthropology as their major. In cases where an anthropology course is aimed at majors in another field (e.g., engineering), setting up and running the course will build capacity within the department for articulating the value of anthropology to students majoring in other disciplines.

- Create a course assignment to evaluate the effectiveness of any new strategy to boost enrollment and retain students

- Develop summer programs or camps focusing on anthropology for pre-first-year students

- Offer a survey course to first-year students on <u>practitioner careers and their impact</u>

- Develop a first-year research program where undergraduates do research led by instructors

- Offer first-year seminars or living/learning communities featuring experiential learning

- Create introductory courses for undecided students, with emphases on interdisciplinarity and applying an anthropological approach (e.g., induction, comparison, emic perspective) in diagnosis and problem solving

- Design courses aimed at other majors (e.g., engineering, premed, law/criminal justice, agriculture, health sciences)

- Offer early access to ethnographic fieldwork, archaeology digs, and lab-based work (e.g., forensic anthropology) and courses that include field trips, community research projects, and ethnographic assignments

- Create themed courses on popular topics

- Invite practitioners, including <u>alumni</u>, to offer a series of workshops on the methods they use in their work

- Develop certificate courses that students can take outside the major

- Collaborate with other departments to mount joint or co-taught courses

- Work with the Honors College to develop new courses

2. Relationship Building

On-campus Activities - These activities will publicize anthropology across your campus and help establish good working relationships with a variety of university influencers and gatekeepers. Most need to be done regularly, not sporadically, to have any real effect. Such efforts must be carefully managed for quality control. Lessons from these encounters should be shared and discussed with the department at large so that the most effective activities are retained.

- Familiarize yourself with the first-year induction programs, find places for anthropology, and get involved—particularly in the first-year orientation

- Develop hands-on experiences for new student orientation (e.g., cultural simulations, archaeology digs)

- Partner with International Student Service office and speak to international students when they arrive on campus

- Partner with pre-health, pre-law and business programs to promote anthropology either as a supplement/enhancement or as a minor

- Visit advisors in other departments to familiarize them with anthropology, learn how students choose courses and majors, and seek advice on pitching anthropology's value to students

- Build smaller communities within the department based on cohort, degree sought, interest areas, or participation in anthropology clubs; consider regular coffee breaks, pizza lunches, game nights, guest speakers, and local field trips

- Ask first-year students if they have a subfield interest and if so, arrange for them to speak with juniors, seniors, or graduate students in that subfield and/or visit local field sites with them

- Ask current anthropology students to take the lead in speaking to student groups

- Identify students taking anthropology-adjacent courses (e.g., religious studies, Latin American studies) and invite them to take anthropology

- Advise student anthropology clubs to devote some of their meetings to job search skills including how to <u>network and conduct informational interviews</u>

- Require all students, instructors, and staff to develop <u>a LinkedIn profile</u> to link with your <u>department's LinkedIn group</u>

- Invite your alumni to link their LinkedIn profile to your <u>department's LinkedIn group</u>; stay in touch with them for student networking, mentoring, career advice, internships, guest lectures, and co-teaching

- Bring <u>alumni</u> back to campus for university-wide events which connect their success to their training in your department

- Volunteer during prospective student days on campus to introduce students and their parents to anthropology

- Encourage students to participate in campus career fairs so they will learn to <u>interact effectively with employers</u>

Off-campus Activities - As with the activities listed above, the goal here is twofold: 1) improve anthropology's presence outside the department, and 2) establish and build working relationships with people and organizations that can help you. Effective planning and consistent, long-term efforts will work.

- Develop first-year engagement programs with various anthropology initiatives at the national, regional and community levels (e.g., Lambda Alpha)

- Create service learning or civic engagement partnerships where students can apply anthropology in local communities

- Collaborate with museums and cultural organizations to 1) provide hands-on experience, 2) offer direct feedback to those organizations based on what the students observe

- Create <u>an alumni network</u> and ask alumni to help you recruit prospective students through their networks

- Participate in career fairs locally, regionally and nationally to understand how they work; then prepare students to interact with the organizational representatives there

- Get involved in one or more organizational or community projects where anthropology students can get supervised hands-on experience and be seen as useful

- Collaborate with the Career Center on <u>student internship placements and funding</u>, alumni contacts, career advising, and job search strategies

- Get to know the local media on campus and in the community and repeatedly pitch stories to them

- Develop relationships with guidance counselors at the high schools in your region, providing them with anthropology marketing materials

- Develop and deliver workshops, seminars and presentations to improve awareness of anthropology to high school students and teachers, especially those offering social science or world history courses

- Establish a student ambassador corps that speaks with high school and community college students about majoring or minoring in anthropology

3. Marketing and Public Outreach

Strategy - Seek advice from experienced campus professionals with resources before embarking on any major initiative. Work with your Career Center, Admissions Office, University Marketing, and Press Office to promote your department, tapping into their resources and advice.

Expansion of Department Website - Your website represents a key opportunity to promote your department to prospective students and their parents, current students, and other key stakeholders (e.g., alumni). It should demonstrate instructor expertise on current issues, project confidence in the department's multifaceted approach to learning (e.g., coursework, internships, project work), and convey student interest and excitement.

- Gather input from current students and alumni to inform your website design, devoting pages to what they consider to be of significant value

- Incorporate images of department members engaged in working together on projects, fieldwork, presentations, learning in the classroom, field, study groups, and online, and practicing new skills

- Allocate separate pages to Bachelor, Master's and PhD students, giving them responsibility for soliciting, creating, and arranging the content

- Dedicate a page to alumni career profiles and their career advice to current students; these brief descriptions can fulfill an undergraduate course assignment that requires interviews and documentary research

- Provide specific examples of how Bachelor, MA, and PhD graduates apply their anthropology training in their work roles

- List available statistics on the types of work anthropology graduates do

- Incorporate testimonials from service learning providers and internship hosts of current students, as well as employers of program graduates

- Using examples, introduce current instructors involved with public affairs, concerns, and issues

- Devote time and energy to refreshing the website content and keeping dates and deadlines up to date

Update Existing Materials - Ensure that all department materials are appealing and responsive to student needs and interests.

- Give your courses intriguing titles and descriptions to emphasize "real-world" problem solving and contemporary issues so that students can relate to them

- Specify the skills (e.g., public presentation, writing open-ended questions, producing/submitting a blogpost or op-ed) incorporated into each course

- Use clear and engaging language to describe courses and programs, avoiding jargon

- Review your materials for attractiveness and consistency

- Make sure your courses are highly visible on all platforms available to students

Create New Materials - Different materials speak to different audiences with distinctive needs. Your messages should stress anthropology's usefulness, relevance, and insight, along with its applicability to entry level jobs and career success.

- Design a "roadmap" or visual plan that illustrates the distinctive features of your program including the domains of knowledge, skills, and experiential learning students acquire; share it widely with prospective students and their parents, majors, administrators, and employers

- Create program materials which are student-friendly and student-oriented

- Set up a student project to design promotional materials featuring students; consider using brochures, videos, talks, web pages, PowerPoints, and/or posts

- Develop parent-oriented materials that highlight knowledge acquisition, skill development, career readiness, alumni careers, and average entry-level salaries

- Produce career-focused marketing materials emphasizing anthropology's relevance for many jobs and fields (e.g., public health, cultural resource management, UX research, evaluation)

- Craft marketing materials to distinguish anthropology from other social sciences (e.g., show students working on projects and digs, in conservation or labs) and stressing its usefulness

- Develop op-ed pieces by both students and instructors on current and local events, demonstrating anthropology's perspective, see <u>Teaching with Op-Eds</u>

- Keep students informed on departmental events, club activities, internship opportunities, project work, and field schools (e.g., through email blasts, social media channels, department home page)

Host Events On and Off Campus - These activities portray anthropologists at work. People can learn directly from you on matters of interest and concern. Your goal is to create a coherent image of anthropology on campus and in your community and region. Through regular exposure, the general public acquires familiarity with your work and a better understanding of it.

- Set up contests and competitions (e.g., poster session, fieldwork photos) to raise anthropology's visibility on campus; publicize on social media

- Promote your graduates' accomplishments through university and department lectures, recognition events, and Alumni Day; highlight them on social media and the department website

- Summarize student, instructor, and alumni projects in various media, including departmental and student newsletters

- Reach out to your campus press officer with information highlighting student and instructor research and activities

- Arrange a meeting with your local TV and radio stations to pitch a topic (e.g., Anthropology confronts the assumptions we have about others) tied to a local story or group

17. Addressing Instructor Concerns about Career Readiness

Janelle-Marie Moreno

As members of the Anthropology Career Readiness Network (ACRN), we have spoken with many instructors about integrating career readiness into their courses or programs. During those conversations, we have noticed a range of reactions from curiosity and openness to hesitation, skepticism, and concern.

The latter reactions are understandable. Professors are already navigating heavy teaching loads, limited resources, and competing institutional demands. It is not uncommon for instructors to worry that adding career-focused content could require a major overhaul of their syllabus or compromise the disciplinary integrity of their courses.

This tool was developed to respond to those concerns directly. It offers a series of common objections—some voiced by instructors, others based on recurring concerns we have observed—paired with practical responses and solutions. Our goal is to show that small changes can make meaningful differences for students and support the long-term sustainability of anthropology as an academic discipline.

Objection: Anthropology shouldn't be vocational.

"We're not a technical or pre-professional discipline. We're here to challenge assumptions, not train employees."

We hear you.

You teach anthropology to challenge assumptions, not to prepare students for narrow career tracks. It is about asking deeper questions and critiquing systems. We respect that. However, we also believe helping students apply their anthropological thinking in the world is not vocationalism but teaching meaningful engagement through a wide range of careers. When we treat career readiness that way, we honor both the discipline and our students' need to navigate the future with clarity.

Here are some sobering facts about the opportunities awaiting anthropology graduates:

Employment Statistics for Anthropology Majors

According to data from the <u>Federal Reserve Bank of New York (2023):</u>

- Unemployment rate: ~9.4% (The average across all majors is ~3.9%!)

- Underemployment rate: ~55.9% (Anthropology degree holders employed in positions that do not require a college degree.)

Anthropology is translational, not transactional

Career readiness does not mean reducing anthropology to job training. It means helping students translate anthropological thinking into real-world contexts where it can make a difference. We are not abandoning theory. Instead, we are extending its reach.

We challenge assumptions and systems

Helping students enter the workforce is a way of challenging systems. Career readiness equips them to bring anthropological insights into spaces where they are often missing including government, healthcare, tech, education, and community work.

Our students need us to care

With underemployment rates over 50% for anthropology graduates, students are already working, often in roles that under-utilize their anthropological skills. If we do not help them connect the dots between their education and their future, who will?

Supporting students is supporting the discipline

Anthropology has long engaged with the practical and the political. Since Franz Boas, applied work has been a part of the discipline's heartbeat. Supporting your students' choices in applying anthropology honors that tradition.

Objection: I'm too busy.

"My plate is overflowing."

"I don't have time to supervise internships."

"We don't have a formal internship office in our department or established community partners."

We hear you.

Between preparing lectures, grading, holding office hours, and advising or mentoring students, your teaching responsibilities alone are substantial. Add in research, whether that is conducting fieldwork, developing publications, or applying for grants; and the load grows heavier. Then there is institutional service: faculty meetings, curriculum reviews, and other departmental responsibilities. On top of that, many of you are reviewing manuscripts, serving on committees, organizing conference panels, and/or collaborating on projects.

And for some, these activities are all happening across multiple campuses, along with administrative duties—all of which must be integrated with your personal/family life.

We recognize that your time is deeply stretched. Building career readiness content into your courses and the program may feel like *just one more thing*.

Possible Solutions to Help Students

Collaborate with colleagues

Consider working with other anthropology instructors to share resources or develop a collective approach. This kind of collaboration reduces duplication and distributes the effort.

Use what is already working

Many programs and departments already engage with community partners, alumni, or local employers. Career readiness has the potential to develop easily from those connections and with minimal lift.

Start small

Introducing career readiness does not mean overhauling your syllabus. A guest speaker, short assignments, or in-class discussions about transferable skills can offer students insights into how anthropology connects to viable, impactful careers. ACRN is here to help support your efforts.

- **Guest speakers at your fingertips**
  ACRN currently has about 50 experienced practitioners ready to serve as guest lecturers, workshop facilitators, or speakers for courses, academic programs, or organizational events. Explore our Speaker's Bureau to browse this growing list of volunteers. It allows you to search by area of expertise, region, and availability for virtual or in-person talks.

  Having trouble finding a speaker for a topic you have in mind? Explore ACRN's Networking and Relationship Building page for practical tools and strategies to help you connect with professionals. ACRN has resources for building alumni relationships, engaging with local organizations, and linking students with potential mentors.

- **Integrate short assignments or in-class discussions into your courses to strengthen real-world career readiness**
  View our Newsletter archive for tips and embedded links to helpful materials and step-by-step plans.

  Explore our Career Ready Curriculum page for tools on introducing practice-based learning (e.g., Your Career Ready Coursework Checklist, A Better ANTH 101), orienting students to issues of the day and project work and incorporating skills that employers value. Discover ways to emphasize communication, application, and critical thinking into your courses.

- **Expose students to project work involving a client**
  Rather than treating career readiness as an "add-on," include it in your courses as a project that entails problem solving.

  For example, client-based class projects are not only opportunities to collaborate with a client on a pressing issue, but also for students to learn how to work collaboratively with each other, a type of experience hiring managers seek in job candidates. Additionally, students learn to apply the methods and theory taught in the classroom while investigating and addressing a real-world problem.

  Client-based class projects involve far less work than a new prep. Their value is so high that your course's popularity will likely increase. And, you will find these class projects both intellectually interesting and fun!

The good news is that you do not have to start from scratch! Review our <u>Class Projects</u> page for ideas on types of clients, projects, and outcomes.

Other benefits accrue as well, since these kinds of projects:

- **Promote the department and institution** through visible, organizational and community-centered work

- **Raise awareness of anthropology's relevance** as a thoughtful, action-oriented discipline

- **Engage students in problem solving** so that they become acquainted with a specific context and the process of developing actionable solutions

- **Build student confidence and marketability** by developing transferable, real-world skills

- **Strengthen institutional ties** with local organizations and businesses.

These efforts can ripple outward by enhancing your program's visibility and helping the applied anthropology community gain the recognition it deserves.

Objection: My students aren't asking for this.

"If they wanted career advice or internships, they'd go to Career Services. They haven't brought it up."

We hear you.

You are already attuned to your students' needs through their questions, their work, and their presence in class. When no one brings up careers or internships, it is easy to assume students are not looking for that kind of support or that they will seek it elsewhere. And with everything else you are managing, it can feel unreasonable to be expected to anticipate unspoken needs or introduce conversations that students themselves are not initiating.

In a sense, we are giving voice to what your students may not understand until later, specifically ***what they wish they had known to ask while in their program***. We are inviting you to help make anthropology classes and programs more career-ready, not by doing more, but by making small, intentional adjustments to the work you have already been doing.

Possible Solutions to Help Students

Make no assumptions

- **They do not know what they do not know**
  Students are typically not aware of the career possibilities open to them, _the kind of work anthropologists do_, or how they might apply their training in any given position. If they have never seen anthropology in action, they may not even know what to ask.

- **Silence ≠ Disinterest**
  A lack of questions does not mean a lack of need or interest. Just as we cannot know the personal histories each anthropology student carries, we also cannot know the reasons behind their silence about the future.

  Some students, especially first-generation college students, are told that their futures are secure simply because they have attained the education that their parents or other family members did not. Then, once they have graduated, they are "gobsmacked" by the realities of the job market.

  Other students may feel isolated in their uncertainty or believe it is inappropriate to discuss their career aspirations. Still others may quietly envision the classic academic ladder: research assistant, future colleague, maybe even department chair. And some believe, conversely, that anthropology is not supposed to lead to a career at all.

  Unspoken assumptions—whether rooted in hope, exposure, confidence, or confusion—deserve to be acknowledged and gently unpacked. The classroom is the safest place for this kind of exploration, because encountering reality after graduation can be disorienting, discouraging, and sometimes devastating. Caring for them while they are matriculating will help them navigate an uncertain future. Bringing career conversations into the classroom helps break the silence, challenge assumptions, and create space for possibility.

Educate Career Services on campus

Campus Career Services can offer general job market preparation, but they cannot articulate how methods like participant observation or critical theory translate into fields such as consulting, public health, user experience, or AI.

Discussions with Career Services can help you learn to advocate for anthropology. This tool, <u>Explaining Anthropology to People in Your Life</u>, may prove useful in those conversations.

Begin with small steps for a big impact

A five-minute story, an alumni visit, or a brief moment to reflect on how anthropological skills transfer to other fields can shift a student's trajectory. Hearing from a real-world anthropologist or a degree-holding anthropology graduate thriving in medicine, law or another field helps students imagine themselves in a career in concrete, grounded ways. Their future is no longer abstract or unrealistic; it becomes tangible and within reach. These moments do not just help to clarify what the future may hold; they affirm students' place in it.

Objection: This isn't my job.

"My role is to teach theory and critical thinking—not to prepare students for careers."

"We don't have a formal internship office in our department or established community partners."

"We don't have the infrastructure."

We hear you.

You became a scholar to pursue your intellectual passions, not to serve as a career counselor. The idea of "job prep" might feel like a mismatch with your training or mission-creep into something outside of your lane. We understand the instinct to protect your time and your disciplinary integrity. That is why any career readiness changes we propose are not about asking you to become something else. Instead, they are about making space in what you already do and connecting it more clearly to your students' futures.

Possible Solutions to Help Students

Bridge theory to action

Preparing students for real-world impact deepens their understanding and ability to apply theory. Applied and career-oriented activities can complement critical thinking by asking students to *use* anthropological frameworks in real-world situations to address problems in organizations and communities.

Start from where you are

No formal infrastructure? No problem. ACRN can offer turnkey materials, guest speakers, and guidance for first steps. Career Services on your campus can assist with finding and sometimes funding internships, so that students see how their classroom learning connects to the world.

Collaborate rather than carry it alone

Career preparation does not have to fall on one person's shoulders. Invite alumni to speak. Partner with colleagues or student clubs. Use ACRN as a hub for shared resources and external support.

Disciplinary strength, not mission drift

Helping students recognize how anthropological thinking applies beyond academia strengthens, not weakens, the discipline. In fact, it is part of anthropology's legacy to engage with the world as it is and to imagine what it could be.

And we're here to **<u>support you</u>**!

18. A Career Ready Curriculum

Riall W. Nolan

Anthropology departments are recognizing the need to address practice in their programs, but historically, there has not been a systematic way of teaching practice. **A Career Ready Curriculum**[1], as presented by the Anthropology Career Readiness Network, provides a framework for introducing practice into your curriculum. These elements do not replace core anthropological training, but instead build on their foundation. This framework is intended to prepare students for practice, but academic-track students will also benefit from career-focused training.

This curriculum "wheel" is a guide to embedding career readiness into a department's existing curriculum. The **hub** of the wheel reflects the traditional core anthropological training as offered by most existing programs. The **spokes** of the wheel represent extensions and enhancements of the traditional anthropology curriculum, designed to highlight career readiness, represented by the 12 elements below. Finally, the **outer rim** of the wheel represents a recent modification to the model. It lists the various modalities through which students learn these elements, ranging from individualized learning through traditional classes, work groups, class projects, and work with outside partners or programs

Elements of the Curriculum

1. **Theory-Practice Connection:** A solid grounding in both theory and practice and their interface enables the application of theory to problem solving and the generation of theory from practice settings

2. **History of Practice:** Learning how practice developed will help students understand potential career options and their evolution

3. **Methods Linked to Problem Solving:**

    - A problem focus helps demonstrate potential use and relevance

    - Future anthropologists need to be equipped with a wider variety of methods than are currently being taught

4. **Domains of Practice:** Exposure to anthropological work (e.g., in non-profits, government, medical) and the issues in those sectors enable students to imagine and explore their own potential paths

5. **Ethics of Practice:** Discussing and debating solutions to common workplace challenges is a good introduction to likely future situations

6. **Promotion of Change:**

    - Teaching theories of change in communities and organizations rarely occurs despite the importance of plans, programs, and policies

    - Being able to translate findings, and plan, implement, and manage change processes, position practitioners to be responsive leaders

7. **Communication**: Presenting to and writing for diverse audiences, including explaining anthropology's relevance and usefulness, are indispensable workplace skills

8. **Practical Experience:** Students need to practice what they have learned (e.g., via internships, class projects) to gain proficiency

9. **Career Planning and Professional Skills:** Students derive significant benefit from collaborating with their peers, managing a project or program, putting networking to work, preparing a resume, or learning to mediate or resolve conflict

10. **Product-oriented Capstone Courses:** Creating a tangible product demonstrates how anthropological knowledge and skills can be put to work; the product can be featured on one's resume

11. **Exposure to Practice and Practitioners:** Inviting alums or local practitioners to speak with students enables students to explore career options and get their questions addressed

12. **Building Networks:** Teaching students how to network, conduct informational interviews, and become part of professional communities significantly increases the likelihood of securing a job

Reference

1. Nolan, Riall W. and Elizabeth K. Briody. 2023. "A Career Ready Curriculum for Anthropologists," *Practicing Anthropology*, 45(3): 26-30, Summer, 2023. <u>DOI: 10.17730/0888-4552.45.3.26</u>.

19. Improving Curriculum Design with the Training Matrix

Riall W. Nolan

ACRN developed a <u>Career Ready Curriculum</u> template for integrating career readiness into a department's curriculum, illustrated by a hub-and-spoke graphic. This tool provides some suggestions for implementing curricular changes, with more detail found in this article.[1]

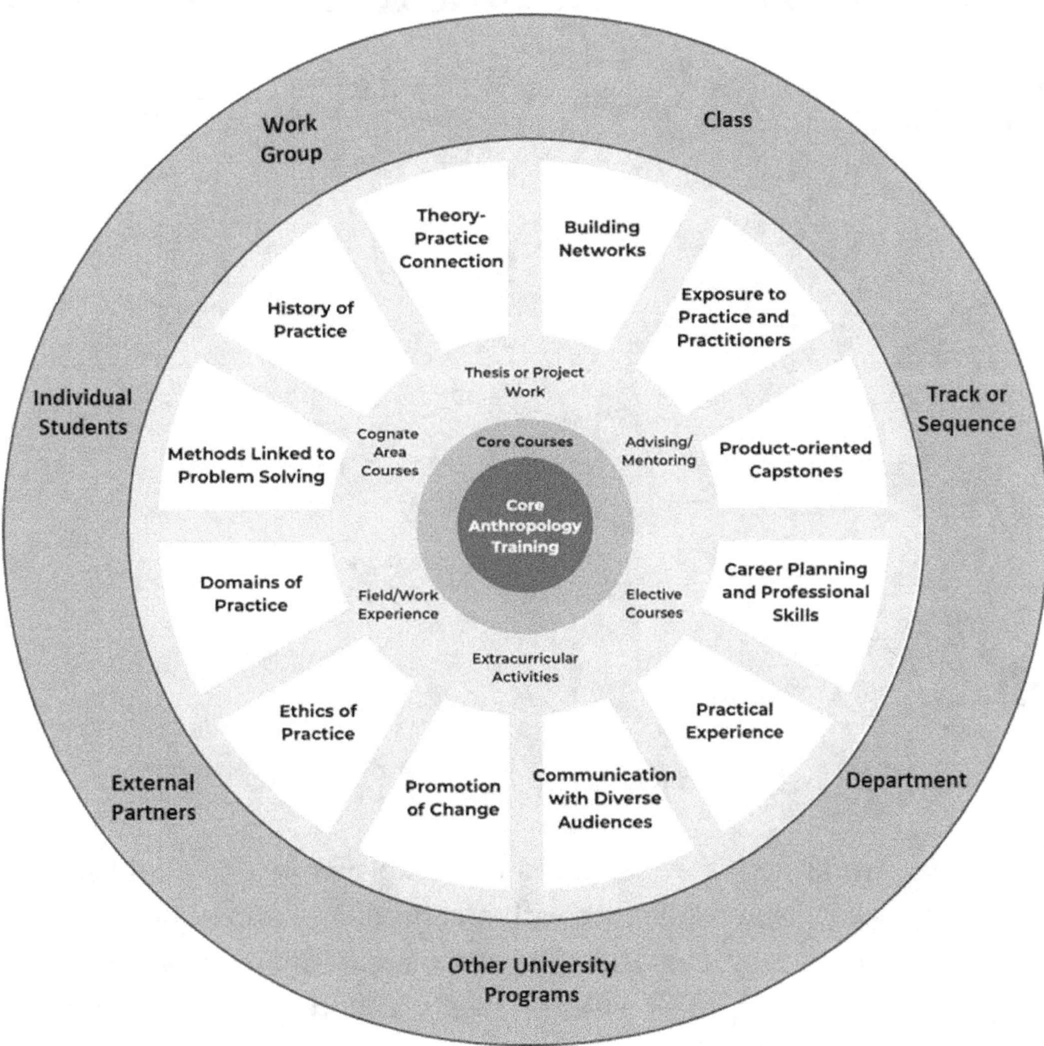

The hub, or core, includes elements found in most academic anthropology programs. The spokes represent additional elements important for practitioner training, which either enhance, extend, or otherwise improve existing features of the curriculum, or which are entirely new. The outer rim of the diagram lists some of the more important modalities through which students learn, ranging from individualized learning through traditional classes, work groups, class projects, and work with outside partners or programs. Any given university course will probably feature several of these modalities.

We developed a simple training matrix combining these learning modalities with the 12 elements of the Career Ready Curriculum, as well as some specific examples of how this information might appear in an enhanced curriculum.

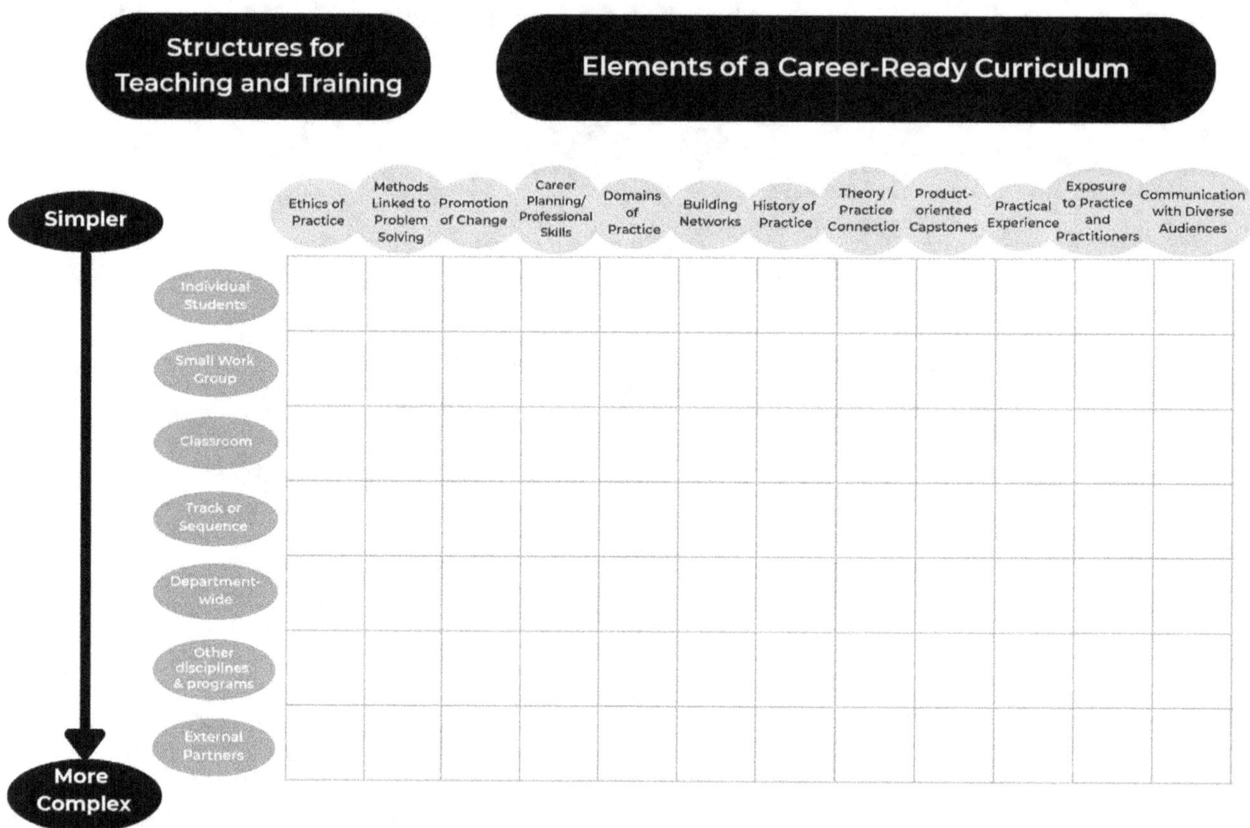

The Training Matrix

The training matrix works both as a planning and an explanatory device. It helps instructors to incorporate knowledge and experience with practice into the existing curriculum. It also helps departments understand the strengths, weaknesses, and gaps in their offerings, as they develop their ability to meet student needs and respond to emerging external challenges and opportunities.

Its purpose is to provide a way of thinking about where and how career-ready elements might be incorporated into an existing curriculum. The horizontal axis of the matrix lists the 12 career-ready elements. The vertical axis shows where and how those elements might be fit in, beginning with individual students and moving to larger and larger units. As the scope of activity increases, so does its complexity.

Possible Matrix Activities

Individual Students: Students work alone on papers or research assignments, conduct interviews with organizational and community members, deliver a class or conference presentation, publish a paper, or participate in a study abroad program.

Work Group: Small groups of three to six students work together on readings, a class discussion, or research assignment. They engage in group problem solving or design exercises. They write a joint proposal, deliver a joint class or conference presentation, or publish a paper together.

Entire Class: Courses are centered specifically on aspects of practice (e.g., domains of work, ethics, design, project management, methods). Modules within a class are focused on some aspect of practice. Class assignments include research, essay writing, and presentation. Class projects with outside organizations occur. Mixed classes (e.g., engineering and anthropology students, anthropology and nursing students) bring distinct groups of students and instructors together.

Track or Sequence: Several courses on aspects of practice are combined into a sequence (e.g., research design, methods, project design, proposal writing, project management). These courses can be part of a track, a major, or a certificate within the department.

Department-wide: An emphasis on application and practice is part of the department's identity. The website and mission reflect the value and relevance of practice. The advising procedures focus on jobs in industry, government, and nonprofits. A robust internship program is in place along with linkages with outside organizations, and frequent talks and workshops by alumni and practitioners.

Other Disciplines and Programs: The department has connections with other programs and activities on campus which can support and enhance its own practice-oriented training.

Credit arrangements are offered for cognate courses, joint courses, or activities with other programs. Collaborative research or grant opportunities are possible.

External Organizations and Partners: The department can tap into internship or practicum opportunities for students with outside organizations, often through campus Career Services. The department has research and application projects with groups and organizations in the community, enabling students to gain valuable problem solving and client management experience.

The training matrix can be adapted in different ways to prepare students for the careers they seek. It connects students with organizational issues and employment beyond the university. It helps instructors plan for and assess how students learn on their own, in collaborative situations, and in external-facing project opportunities.

Reference

1. Nolan, Riall W. and Elizabeth K. Briody. 2023. "A Career Ready Curriculum for Anthropologists," *Practicing Anthropology*, 45(3): 26–30, Summer.

20. Your Career Ready Coursework Checklist

Elizabeth K. Briody

Anthropology instructors often ask how they might integrate career readiness into their courses. The Coursework Checklist identifies a variety of course activities; it can be used in tandem with the tool <u>Bringing Anthropological Practice into the Classroom</u>.

Why Checklists?

Checklists have many purposes:

- **Raise awareness** of activities to introduce career readiness

- **Motivate instructors** to incorporate career readiness into anthropological training

- **Ensure student exposure** to these activities

- **Communicate the value** of career readiness to students and administrators

- **Measure progress over time** in institutionalizing career readiness activities

Coursework Checklist

The Coursework Checklist includes common career readiness activities for existing as well as potential undergraduate and graduate courses. Most of these activities involve experiential learning; some require interaction. As a rule, no particular sequence of these activities is necessary. However, the activities are arranged to correspond generally with the key stages in students' <u>career journeys</u>.

The Checklist is structured into two parts:

- Engagement with Industry, Nonprofit and Government Employees

- Career Readiness Exercises

Numerous <u>Job Seeker and Career Tools</u> are available on the ACRN website. The ACRN Workbook *Career Tools for Anthropology*, available in paperback or e-book, offers specific exercises to reinforce career readiness learning.

Instructions

Use this Coursework Checklist to identify the number of times you included career readiness activities in your courses during the last term. This process helps you to establish your baseline. Score and sum each part of the Checklist separately and then calculate the overall total.

Track your progress by completing this Coursework Checklist each term. Then set new goals for incorporating additional career readiness activities into your courses in the future. The following scale can serve as a guide.

Urgent Need for Career Readiness (Score = 0)

- No career readiness activities in place

Limited Career Readiness (Score = 1-3)

- Occasional alumni guest speakers
- Capstone products include a resume and portfolio
- Career panel held three years ago

Moderate Career Readiness (Score = 4-7)

- Two courses carry out client-based class projects each term
- New professionalization course taught once
- Department roadmap being created
- Department LinkedIn Group launched with invitations sent to several alumni

Robust Career Readiness (Score = 8+)

- Numerous career activities integrated into 80% of semester coursework
- A Department career panel and practitioner workshop each term
- Required UG and grad student participation in certain Career Services events
- All UG students reliably secure at least one internship

Engagement with Industry, Nonprofit, and Government Employees (including Practitioners and Alumni)	# of times during the last term?
• as guest speakers and/or panelists	
• as workshop presenters	
• as interviewees	
• as clients for a class project	
• as supervisors for student projects	
• as internship supervisors	
• Other (specify)	
Total	

Career Readiness Exercises	# of times during the last term?
Require students to develop their LinkedIn profiles	
Teach students to recognize the skills they possess and how to translate their skills for the workplace	
Assign students to investigate one or more career domains	
Have students practice using at least three data collection methods	
Introduce students to methodological skills used in many workplaces	
Have students practice using at least two data analysis methods	
Partner with an organization on an issue it wants to address; conduct a client-based class project that provides recommendations to the organization	
Work with individual students on a client-based project	
Require students to give a presentation	
Assign students to write a blogpost, perhaps for ACRN's World of Work Blog	
Assign students to write an op-ed article	
Assign students to write a policy brief or craft a new policy for an organization or community	
Teach students the basics of networking and have them practice initiating contact with professionals they want to meet	
Assign students to conduct an informational interview with a practitioner on their own, in pairs, or as a class; ask the practitioner to review the resulting career profile and then post it on the Department website's career page	
Expect students to review what campus Career Services offers and prepare specific questions for a Career Services guest speaker	
Expect students to sign up for potential job opportunities at campus Career Services	

Career Readiness Exercises	# of times during the last term?
Require students to develop and rehearse their elevator pitch with one or more partners, integrating key feedback	
Teach students that employers look for job candidates who are problem solvers and that their resumes should highlight their problem solving experience	
Require students to develop a resume which emphasizes "outcomes," the impact of their actions on groups and organizations	
Have students craft a cover letter	
Require students to participate in mock interviews using the STAR method	
Other (specify)	
Total	
Grand Total of Career Readiness Activities	

21. A Better ANTH 101

Michael Wesch, Aimee Huard, and Elizabeth K. Briody

Students' first exposure to anthropology typically occurs in an introductory college course on the subject. A key goal for instructors is to engage students and help them see the potential of anthropology in their lives and work. For a variety of reasons (e.g., pressure from legislators and administrators, reduction in General Education requirements), anthropology is struggling to remain a vibrant and viable discipline. This tool outlines three integrated areas of focus with which you can rethink and rebuild your Anthropology 101 course whether you are teaching in person or online:

1. **Inspire students to contemplate big ideas about what it means to be human:** Urge students to explore new viewpoints, interpretations, and questions as they attempt to make sense of the world. Help them learn to open up their minds in new ways.

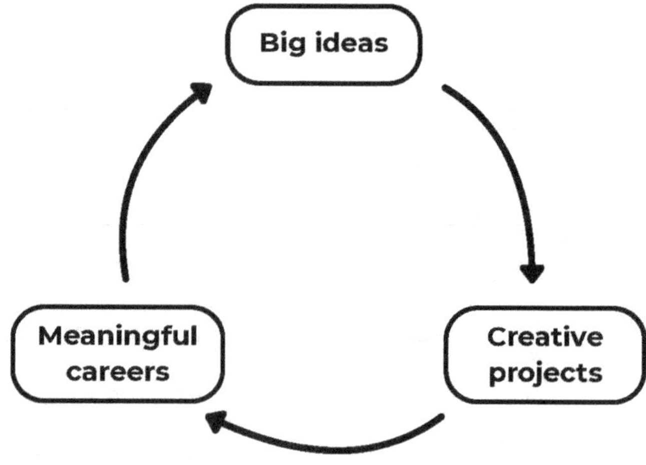

2. **Create projects to put these big ideas into action:** Encourage students to think creatively and apply these concepts through specific projects "out in the world."

3. **Make these big ideas meaningful to their career aspirations:** Help students see the many ways in which anthropology applies to the diversity of work experiences, including their own. Offer examples of anthropology's usefulness and relevance in solving problems in organizations and communities.

Focus 1: Find the Big Ideas

1. Emphasize the *Why.*

Jessica Able (https://jessicaabel.com/xy-story-formula/) studied the best storytellers of our time and came up with a simple and memorable "XY" formula. X is what your story is about whereas Y is why it is interesting. When teaching, anthropologists often focus on a topic (where X = subsistence, language, culture, and political systems, among other domains).

Yet, every X has a Y (a Why)—a reason why it is important to teach. Review the X's (topics) on your syllabus. In every lecture, identify the Y for each topic and make it explicit. The Y's represent your big ideas.

Typically, introductory courses begin with a focus on culture. But why is culture important? What can be done to stimulate mindset shifts? The Y of these early lessons on culture is to get students to lean into difference, get them excited about human diversity, and begin to dismantle some of their own cultural biases to ask questions they have never asked before.

Keeping this Y in mind will put you in an optimal frame of mind to craft lectures, discussions, and activities which will achieve the Why, rather than simply delivering the X information.

You might also consider an "X-Y-Me" formula. Start your class by introducing X (the topic), telling them Y it is important, and at the end asking them to reflect on Me ("This is important to me because …."). Such daily reflections will help you stay in tune with your students, refine your Y's, and possibly discover new X's you want to cover in future classes.

2. Craft your own big ideas.

Your syllabus might still relate to the traditional topics (e.g., language, economics, social organization). However, by identifying and centering the Y for each topic, you are helping your students understand the rationale behind these topics and the new ideas you want them to consider.

An example of this process can be found here (https://anth101.com/). For more details on the Y of each topic, see this free online textbook: *The Art of Being Human*. Feel free to incorporate or modify any of this material for your own classes.

Traditional Textbook Topics	Possible Big Ideas
Culture, Ethnocentrism, and Cultural Relativism	People are different. These differences represent the vast range of human potential and possibility.
The Anthropological Perspective	We can respond to cultural differences with hate or ignorance, or we can choose to open up to them and ask questions we have never considered before.
Human Evolution	When we open up to such questions, we put ourselves in touch with our higher nature. It was asking questions, making connections, and trying new things that brought us down from the trees, and took us to the moon.
Language	It is not easy to see our assumptions. Our fundamental assumptions are embedded in the basic elements of our everyday lives (e.g., language, routines, technologies).
Subsistence and Economy	John Culkin wrote: "We create our tools and then our tools create us." Our technologies and modes of subsistence and economy have profound effects on how we live, organize our families and societies, and even how we think (and vice versa).
Social Organization, Kinship, Descent, Class, Caste, Race, Gender, and Identity	Most of what we take as "reality" is a cultural construction, made real through our unseen, unexamined assumptions of what is right, true, or possible.
*Art and Religion	We fail to examine our assumptions not only because they are hard to see, but also because they are safe and comfortable. They allow us to live with the flattering illusion that "I am the center of the universe, and what matters are my immediate needs and desires."
Globalization, Culture Change, and Structural Power	Our failure to move beyond our assumptions has led to the tragedy of our times: that we are more connected than ever yet feel and act more disconnected.
**What is the Good Life? And how can we achieve it?	Memorizing these ideas is easy. Living them takes a lifetime of practice. Fortunately, the heroes of all time have walked before us. They show us the path, demonstrating that collectively, we make the world. Understanding how we make the world—how it could be made or understood differently—is the road toward realizing our full human potential. It is the road to freedom.

*This section also covers topics that encourage empathic understanding of different perspectives on morality and politics as well as religion and art.

**The last section on What is the Good Life offers an opportunity to share inspiring stories of anthropologists and those influenced by anthropology making a difference in the world in a wide range of fields. (See the work of Edward Fischer.)

Focus 2: Create Out-in-the-World Projects

Projects are intended to align generally with the big ideas you present in class. However, some projects will last longer than others and may be completed after you have introduced other big ideas.

1. Identify Your Goals.

Some projects, known as *"challenges,"* are designed to foster personal growth and change. Challenges can be fun, engaging, and relatively easy to grade (i.e., as "complete/incomplete"), making them suitable for large classes. *Methods-oriented projects* introduce students to anthropological methods (e.g., observation, interviewing) and connect their interests to anthropology. Finally, *skill development projects* help students develop skills (e.g., public speaking, collaboration, problem solving). Figure out how you might integrate a mix of these projects throughout the course.

2. Connect a Big Idea with Potential Projects Out-in-the-World.

Engage students in discussions of a big idea during class so that they have a conceptual foundation for their projects.

- **"Culture, Ethnocentrism, and Cultural Relativism" Example:** Your big idea on culture is to get students excited about human differences, lean into and appreciate them, and learn from them. A simple, yet challenging, project is to talk to a stranger. The student must meet a stranger, hear that person's story, and ask to share it with their classmates.
- **"The Anthropological Perspective" Example:** This big idea highlights how anthropologists approach understanding and explaining human behavior using ethnographic methods. Have your students work in pairs to observe activity in a bookstore, gym, public park, or sports event, noting specific event sequences and documenting what they observed. Once each pair has reconciled any differences, they report on what was challenging about the assignment and what findings they found most surprising.

3. Decide on the Number of Projects.

For a semester-based course, you probably have time for about eight short projects—about one every two weeks—or one long project with scaffolding to aid students in doing anthropology (the process) as much as the final product.

- **Short Project Example:** Students complete at least one hour of fieldwork, immersing themselves in a cross-cultural or sub-cultural experience—a place, event, or activity that makes them uncomfortable. Then students write up a "thick description" (i.e., context, behaviors) of their experience.
- **Long Project Example:** Try an "un-essay" to encourage student creativity. Students pick a topic to investigate; the final product cannot be an essay. For example, the product might be a short video, PowerPoint, or podcast. Un-essays help students connect their passions to academics using the broader themes of anthropology as a foundation. Critical to the project are individual check-ins to keep students on track, self-reflections to connect the project to anthropology, and self-reflections on their process of doing the project.

4. Make Projects Worth Doing.

Ask yourself, "Would I want to do this? Is it so fun or interesting or useful that I want to do it again and again?" If the answer is yes, it is a good assignment.

- **Challenges Examples:** Several examples can be found here (https://anth101.com/).
  - A student favorite is "The 28 Day Challenge" to break a habit or learn something new in 28 days while reflecting on our evolutionary ability to learn and create habits.
  - Another is "The UnThing Challenge" in which students give up a key technology for a week to explore how technology influences our lives.
  - A third is called "The Other Encounter." Each student finds an "other" who holds different political or religious beliefs and challenges them to empathize across big differences. Many students report doing these assignments again and again on their own long after the course is over because they find them important to their own growth and development.
- **Un-essay Examples:** Submissions may vary from a dramatic poetry reading based on a Cherokee wedding legend, to an investigation into the Icelandic knitting tradition in modern culture, to a ceramicist learning a new technique based on ancient Greek practices. When students present their projects to the class, the range of final products is just as interesting to them as it is to their professor.

5. Incorporate Reflection into Project Work.

Regular reflections on the process of the project, and its connections to anthropology, ground the *whys* of the project to the course. Self-reflections emphasize the importance of process over product, illustrating how the journey of the project unfolding entails critical thinking, decision making, and evaluation. Individual check-ins can help keep larger, multi-component projects on track.

6. Make Projects Fun to Share.

Great projects usually result in a product that students enjoy sharing. Students are eager to lead a class discussion about their project experiences as well as listen to their classmates' stories. These varied experiences and approaches allow students to engage in critical reflection, as well as build rapport by supporting their classmates' work.

Focus 3: Make Anthropology Meaningful in Your Career

Exposing students to the work of anthropologists represents the third feature of a revitalized introductory course. Anthropologists work as practitioners in industry, nonprofits, and government where they are employed to address a variety of issues—from climate change to consumers, and from consulting to cultural resource management. Use these suggestions to align anthropologists' careers or work with your big ideas.

1. Raise awareness of anthropology's usefulness.

Have students watch "Increase Public Awareness," the fifth video from *Anthropologists on the Public Stage*. (They will have to register first to view any of the six videos.) It highlights examples of anthropologists sharing their training and insights publicly. The exercise accompanying the fifth video is designed to get students to imagine one way in which they could help others learn about anthropology and why it has value in society.

2. Introduce students to anthropologists at work.

For each big idea, introduce a career profile (e.g., Gillian Tett with "Globalization, Cultural Change, and Structural Power;" Helen Fisher with "Social Organization, Kinship, Descent, Class, Caste, Race, Gender, and Identity"). Discuss their expertise, skills, life experiences, and careers. Separately, use sNAPAshots to show anthropologists talking about a wide range of careers.

3. Help students make the connections.

Hold frequent discussions about how anthropology is already helping them in their daily lives and of how it might assist them in their future careers. Have students explore possible careers using their anthropological training. Invite practitioners into your class as guest speakers; consider ACRN's Speaker's Bureau as a source. Other strategies include establishing connections with local organizations, your department's alumni, or using LinkedIn to connect with your alumni.

4. Ask students to create alumni career profiles.

Assign a student or pair of students to read about and then interview a graduate of your department. This assignment has the virtue of acquainting students with background research on the alum, the interview process, and the creation of a final career profile. It gives students a chance to practice and internalize what they are learning (e.g., interview methods, career knowledge). When pairs of students are involved, this task exposes them to the challenges of collaborating with others, a situation they will encounter wherever they work. When these career profiles are posted on your department's website (e.g. https://anthropology.osu.edu/career-profiles), current and future students can access them as part of the department's career resources.

22. Introducing Anthropology in a First-Year Course

Riall W. Nolan

Anthropology faces two linked problems: building enrollments and demonstrating relevance to students. A first-year undergraduate course showing students what anthropology can do in the world can help address both issues.

Giving first-year students a look at how anthropology is used by practitioners in a variety of different arenas will help students understand the discipline better. It also will show them how and why what they are learning can be used once they are in the workplace. Most importantly, it demonstrates anthropology's problem-solving capabilities.

This tool offers an outline for the design of a first-year course in how anthropology works in the world. It can be easily adapted to a variety of academic structures and calendars[1].

The course is structured into three parts:

- **Part One** covers some basic information about anthropology.

- **Part Two** looks in some detail at specific domains of practice, and what anthropologists do there.

- **Part Three** takes up some important questions and issues regarding practice.

Students who take this course will come away with a clear understanding of how relevant anthropological training can be in a wide variety of situations to tackle problems large and small. It will be useful to them the next time someone asks, *"Interesting, but _what is anthropology good for?"_*

Structure

The following structure is based on a 16-week semester calendar but can be adapted for other timeframes.

Part One: Weeks 1-4

Since this course is designed to be a first-year offering, the first part focuses on **the discipline of anthropology**, with an emphasis on a few key methods, how the methods are used, and the history of application and practice in anthropology.

- Basic course information
- Anthropology as a discipline: defining characteristics
- Key anthropological methods
- The use of methods in practice
- The history of application in anthropology
- How practitioners are trained
- How practice differs from university-based anthropology.

Part Two: Weeks 5-14

The second and main part of the course is devoted to looking at some of the principal **domains of activity** in which anthropologists play an important role. The coverage of domains can vary somewhat from year to year, but for each domain, it is essential to describe what anthropologists do in the area and the main issues or challenges they face. For each domain, the emphasis is on how anthropology helps to solve problems. Suggested domains include:

- Health
- Military and national security
- International development
- Business
- Marketing
- Design
- Environment
- Disaster and Humanitarian Relief
- AI and Cyberculture
- User Experience Research.

Part Three: Weeks 15-16

The third and final section of the course takes up some of the main questions and issues relating to anthropological practice. It shows students how anthropology is used both at a highly professionalized level (i.e., with a PhD) and by people with a BA or MA degree. Topics include:

- The ethics of practice
- The training of practitioners
- The nature of practitioner careers
- The future impact of anthropology.

Pedagogy

Readings are assigned in advance of each class meeting. A short 10-question quiz can be given once a week on the week's material. Lectures are combined with group discussions based either on the readings assigned or on key questions suggested either by the students or the instructor. Students submit two 3,000-word essays for grading, one halfway through the class and the other in lieu of a final exam.

Part Two is structured differently than the rest of the course. Each week is devoted to a single domain of practice. The first class session outlines the nature of the domain and the work that anthropologists do in that domain. The second session usually involves a conversation with a practitioner working in that domain, either through a classroom visit or a video call. An alternate option is to assign specific articles by a practitioner describing their work. The third and final session is a wrap-up discussion of issues and questions arising.

Assignments

In addition to the weekly quizzes, students write two 3,000-word essays. Here are the topics and prompts.

FIRST ESSAY: WHAT IS PRACTICING ANTHROPOLOGY AND WHY SHOULD WE CARE?

Pretend you are working in an organization. You pick the organization. Based on that organization's work and future agenda, write an extended memo to the executive board outlining what practicing anthropology is, why it is useful and important, and why they should hire a practitioner immediately.

Provide an annotated bibliography, so that if they want to read more, they can.

SECOND ESSAY: WHAT DOES ANTHROPOLOGY CONTRIBUTE TO A PARTICULAR DOMAIN OF APPLICATION?

Choose a domain of anthropological application. It can be one of the ones that we discussed in class, or another one. Write an essay of no more than 3,000 words (exclusive of references), in which you:

1. Describe the domain, what it does, and how it operates
2. Describe how anthropology works in this domain
3. Analyze the contribution of anthropology to both the domain and to the discipline, and
4. Discuss key problems or issues arising from anthropology's involvement.

Readings

A large and diverse literature of practice is available to help supplement this course.

- Artz, Matt and Lora Koycheva, eds. 2025. *EmTech Anthropology: Careers at the Frontier*. New York, NY: Taylor & Francis.

- Briller, Sherylyn H. and Amy Goldmacher. 2021. *Designing an Anthropology Career: Professional Development Exercises*. 2nd ed. Lanham, MD: Rowman & Littlefield.

- Koycheva, Lora, Angela K. VandenBroek, and Matt Artz, eds. 2026. *Anthropology and AI*. London, UK: Routledge.

- Nolan, Riall W., ed. 2013. *A Handbook of Practicing Anthropology*. Malden, MA: Wiley-Blackwell.

- Nolan, Riall W. 2003. *Anthropology in Practice: Building a Career Outside the Academy*. Boulder, CO: Lynne Rienner Publishers.

- Nolan, Riall W. 2026. *Using Anthropology in the World: A Guide to Becoming an Anthropologist Practitioner*. London, UK: Taylor & Francis.

- Redding, Terry M. and Charles C. Cheney, eds. 2022. *Profiles of Anthropological Praxis: An International Casebook*. New York, NY: Berghahn.

- Strang, Veronica. 2021. *What Anthropologists Do*. 2nd ed. London, UK: Routledge.

- Trester, Anna Marie. 2022. *Employing Linguistics: Thinking and Talking about Careers for Linguists*. London, UK: Bloomsbury Academic.

- Wasson, Christina, ed. 2026. *Routledge Handbook of Applied Anthropology*. London, UK: Routledge.

- Wasson, Christina, Mary Odell Butler, and Jacqueline Copeland-Carson, eds. 2012. *Applying Anthropology in the Global Village*. Walnut Creek, CA: Left Coast Press.

- Wulff, Robert M. and Shirley J. Fiske, eds. 1987. *Anthropological Praxis: Translating Knowledge into Action*. Boulder, CO: Westview Press.

Other Resources

- ACRN's Speaker's Bureau includes the names and career profiles of anthropologists working in industry, nonprofits, and government. These individuals are available for video and in-person classroom presentations, workshops, conferences, and other events.

- ACRN has developed Job Seeker tools that pertain directly to specific careers. Students can connect directly with alumni from their institutions by using LinkedIn to connect with them. Many other resources available on the ACRN website, including the tool Explaining Anthropology to People in Your Life.

- The National Association for the Practice of Anthropology offers sNAPAshots, brief videos showcasing anthropologists talking about their careers.

- The six short videos and exercises in Anthropologists on the Public Stage are worth exploring. (Users will need to register first to view the videos). The fifth video, "Increase Public Awareness," offers examples of anthropologists sharing their training and insights publicly.

Reference

1. This course is based in large part on a course that Riall Nolan designed and taught at Purdue University.

23. Promoting Courses with a Dash of Pop Culture

Emma Pramuk

What if it were possible to hook students on anthropology before they took their first class or to pique their interest in your new course? With a catchy title and a *hint* of pop culture, it can become a reality and a way to help boost anthropology enrollments.

Pop culture, or popular culture, refers to the ideas, trends, entertainment, and social practices that are widely accepted and consumed by the general public. Typical elements include music, movies, fashion trends, and even slang. This tool will help you start the brainstorming process to create a "buzz" around your course or upcoming event. And, it will keep it timely since people are more likely to be interested in what catches their attention.

Keys to Creating and Keeping Interest

1. Know Your Audience - Target them!

Start with the end goal: reaching your audience. Are they current anthropology students, undeclared majors, or graduate students? For example, you may want to generate and retain student interest in an introductory anthropology class while also explaining anthropology's importance and relevance.

2. Create a Catchy Title - Keep it fun!

Think of a title like a pitch. Keep it short, but captivating. A persuasive title for an event is three to four words, but feel free to add a five-to-six-word subtitle to let them know what the event is really about. Avoid words that are uncommon. Alliteration, a play on words, and slang are great ways to keep it fun. Titles should be understandable and encourage people to want to know more. A good course title might be: "Culture IRL: Anthropology in Everyday Life." It incorporates *text slang*, "IRL" (i.e., in real life) and then provides a brief subtitle offering additional detail.

3. Incorporate Pop Culture - When possible

Pop culture references not only generate interest, but can also create instant an instant connection for students. If you tie your course and title to a current trend, or incorporate a popular form of media, you will draw their attention. If you are unaware of popular trends, ask your students or do an online search for "Trending Topics." To add relatability to your title, consider these alternatives:

- *Barbie, Beyoncé, and Belonging: Understanding Culture through Representation*

- *Why Is Everything a Vibe? Exploring Culture in Ways that You Can "Feel"*

Of course, not everything needs to be tied into pop culture. This approach works better with some topics than others.

4. Do Your Research - Is it appropriate, relevant, and timely?

Words may have more than one meaning, especially if you are incorporating a pop culture reference. Make sure you research the meaning of your title, so that it will not be misconstrued. A simple online search is a useful starting point, but you might also ask a student, a peer, or a professional for their views. Similarly, when referencing pop culture, do your best to guard against controversy such as some "hidden" meaning in your title.

Ensure that your reference is relevant to the topic, and highlight that relevance in your outreach. You do not want to reference Beyoncé if no mention of her is included in the actual course. For example, you could use an image from one of her videos on your class flyer, and then center a discussion on the video's use of color in your Semiotics course. Song lyrics and short video skits can also help persuade your target audience to attend and keep coming back if they have meaning for them.

Stay current. Advertising slogans from "back in the day" may fall flat on your audience. "This is not your father's Oldsmobile" will not resonate with Gen Z if they have never heard it, or worse, if they do not know what an Oldsmobile is! Other brands link to elements of pop culture. Nike's memorable slogan has enjoyed long-term staying power. What about offering a workshop called "Just Do It: PhotoVoice in Your Research"?

5. Market - You have done the work, so show it off!

Posters and flyers can help promote your course or event! Add fun graphics that make your title pop. <u>Canva</u>, <u>PicsArt</u>, and many other platforms have quick and easy-to-use templates to assist you. Post them to your social media pages or print them out and hang them up around campus. Advertising in this way will get people talking!

24. Bringing Anthropological Practice into the Classroom

Andrew Walsh

Students are often drawn to anthropology by discovering its intriguing potential, even if they do not see an obvious connection to a job upon graduation. Yet, as graduation approaches, the question inevitably arises: <u>What can you do with a degree in anthropology?</u> Anthropology instructors can do better than answering this question with vaguely encouraging platitudes such as, "Whatever you like!"

One approach that has shown great promise is to assign practitioner work in *every* course, not just courses entitled "applied" or "practicing" anthropology. Starting with first-year students, emphasize that much of "anthropology" occurs in workplaces where the majority of students will be employed after securing their degrees: industry, nonprofits, and government. Those workplaces represent a fieldwork frontier, an exploration into the distinctive worlds of organizations, employers, and clients. And, students will appreciate that practitioners use various formats (e.g., publications, videos, presentations, podcasts) to describe their career paths, experiences, and projects.

Why assign or encourage students to learn about the work of practicing anthropologists?

Exposing students to work which involves practical problem solving:

- Allows them to imagine a variety of projects, jobs, or careers they might pursue
- Helps students recognize that organizational leaders seek insights into how their workplaces can become more effective, how they can address user/consumer/patient concerns as well as supplier issues, and how they can contribute to society generally
- Provides students with knowledge of specific cases when presenting the value of anthropological perspectives to others (e.g., hiring managers, colleagues)

- Enables individual study and class discussion on how anthropological perspectives, approaches, methods, and insights are applied in a variety of problem-solving contexts beyond the classroom
- Encourages students to think critically by considering the many factors that enable and/or limit the effectiveness of anthropological approaches to the issues they care about
- Demonstrates to institutions, funders and, most importantly, themselves that anthropology's value includes research but goes beyond it to problem solving and implementation of change
- Helps instructors to consider and keep up to date with practitioner work and trends that they might otherwise miss

Should the research, evaluation, and work experiences of practitioners be confined to courses in "applied" or "practicing anthropology?"

The answer is "No"!

- **Introductory or general education courses:** Instructors might ask students to reflect on how anthropology's foundational concepts and distinctive methods lend themselves to real-world applications. Discussion can include examples of case studies that may have affected students' lives without them even knowing it. With this strategy, instructors help a variety of students learn about anthropology's relevance, not just future anthropology majors or minors. It has the potential of encouraging all students in the class to incorporate anthropological perspectives and insights as they pursue careers in a variety of fields.
- **Advanced, topic-specific courses:** In courses such as Medical Anthropology, Museum Anthropology, Environmental Anthropology, Cultural Resource Management, Business Anthropology and others, students could have assignments to find, read, report on, and debate cases in which anthropological methods and findings have addressed specific issues—say, pertaining to health, heritage, law and policy, and marketing. With this strategy, instructors highlight real-world applications of issues covered in class.
- **Independent study or capstone courses:** Instructors might have students select and examine cases in which anthropological perspectives, approaches and insights have been used in problem solving. Students would follow up by reflecting on how anthropology might be used in tackling other problems. They could also be asked to anticipate and try to address obstacles they are likely to face along the way. With

this strategy, instructors encourage students to envision how they would use their anthropological training no matter what career path they follow.

How do you encourage the relevance of anthropological thinking and approaches for students after graduation?

Help students plan for their future by:

- Introducing them to practitioner work and asking them to write an application essay or memo which communicates the value of their anthropological training in a particular domain of work
- Exploring the work of public figures (e.g., authors, politicians, activists, artists, actors) who have studied anthropology, getting them to discuss how the careers of these individuals may have been informed by anthropology's core lessons
- Assigning selected autoethnographic readings and having students attempt to understand and write about some of their own choices and preferences in an anthropological way

How might students practice some of the ways in which anthropological insights are regularly communicated outside of the classroom?

Formats might include:

- Short, compelling, and accessible articles, posts, graphics, videos, or TED-talk style presentations intended to communicate anthropological insights to a broad public
- Well-informed, op-ed articles that make cogent and convincing evidence-based contributions to ongoing debates around key public issues
- A competition along the lines of the American Anthropology Association's Three-Minute Thesis contest (https://americananthro.org/practice-teach/three-minute-thesis-competition/)
- Briefing reports intended to explain anthropological insights on a specific topic, dilemma, or policy to an audience of non-specialists

Where do you find examples of practitioner research and implementation projects?

- Books advocating this approach include _Anthro-Vision_ (Tett), _Profiles of Anthropological Praxis_ (Redding and Cheney), _Anthropological Praxis_ (Wulff and Fiske), and _Business Anthropology: The Basics_ (de Waal Malefyt)
- Applied journals devoted to this kind of work include _Practicing Anthropology_, _Journal of Business Anthropology_, _Human Organization_, and others
- ACRN class projects highlight some cases which students have translated into Instagram-ready posts and infographics
- Ask a librarian to help students identify sources and contribute to an open access library of anthropology case studies

How do you find practitioners willing to talk about their projects or careers?

- ACRN Speaker's Bureau includes the names of scores of practitioners, their contact information, relevant areas of expertise, and bios
- sNAPAshots are brief career videos of practicing anthropologists which are produced by the National Association for the Practice of Anthropology
- Your program's alumni can be contacted and invited to discuss how anthropology remains relevant to them:
  - Reach out through your university's LinkedIn page and search for anthropology
  - Create a LinkedIn anthropology group for your department and invite alumni to link to it
  - Ask your campus Career Planning Office to help you connect with anthropology alumni
- Podcasts such as Adam Gamwell's This Anthro Life, Anthropology in Business with Matt Artz, and others invite anthropologists to speak on a variety of issues including careers

25. Informational Interviewing in the Classroom

Elizabeth K. Briody

Anthropologists working in industry, nonprofits, and government are role models for students who will someday work those same areas. They are sources of valuable information as students begin making decisions about their job search or continued schooling. Inviting practitioners in person or virtually into the classroom to answer questions about their career path and current work responsibilities will encourage students to imagine their future work opportunities. The lessons from this hands-on experience will instill in your students the confidence to set up informational sessions on their own. These six steps will help them understand the process and the benefits:

- Select practitioners that can offer expertise and a variety of career experiences
- Organize the logistics of the visit
- Prepare and practice the informational interview technique
- Conduct the informational interview
- Debrief and express thanks
- Document the connection as part of one's professional networks

In addition, you are teaching your students to work with each other to complete these tasks, familiarizing them with the expectations surrounding collaboration in most work environments.

Selection

Choosing guest speakers involves a series of decisions.

- **Who chooses the speakers?** Will you identify possible candidates, or will you let your students conduct a search?

- **What criteria matter?** You want each speaker's career to be broadly consistent with the course material (e.g., environment, health, business, heritage management, forensics). Does it matter to you if the speakers are local, or alumni of your program, or able to be present in person? Do you prefer speakers who are seasoned anthropologists compared to recent graduates? And where do your students' preferences fit in?

- **How will the speakers be chosen?** Will you suggest a general internet or LinkedIn search, or consider using ACRN's Speaker's Bureau or NAPA's sNAPAshots? Perhaps you or your students know of some good speakers?

    o Choose one or more sources for finding speakers
    o Re-state the selection criteria
    o Ask students to list the reasons for their preferred speakers
    o Discuss as a class
    o Generate a prioritized list of candidate speakers

- **Lesson:** Making selection decisions, including creating selection criteria, represents the kind of transferable skill that your students will apply in their schooling, work, and lives in general.

Organization

Inviting and securing speakers begins the first week of class.

- **Getting the contact information:** If you do not possess this information, ask two students to find one or more emails and, if possible, a mobile phone number. Some sites provide such detail (e.g., ACRN Speaker's Bureau). Students could search for a professional website or tap LinkedIn for the practitioner's profile page. This ACRN tool on LinkedIn Profile Features and Checklist will introduce students to LinkedIn.

- **Sending the email:** Ask two students to craft an invitational email. The request should include the following:

    o Request for a guest speaker
    o Course name and department
    o Relevance of speaker's background to course and student career interests
    o Event format: Students conduct an informational interview lasting 15-20 minutes with a debrief following
    o Possible dates and time the class meets, including time zone

- - Indication of in person or online
  - Statement about offering a modest honorarium (if available through your department)

Proofread the email and send via your own email.

- **Finalizing the event:** You negotiate any remaining details with the speaker:

  - Revisit event format with associated timing
  - Clarify any questions
  - If in person, make necessary arrangements (e.g., for travel, hotel) and if online, provide the link to connect with the classroom

- **Lesson:** Students learn the key tasks of inviting a guest speaker.

Preparation and Practice

The Technique

- **Definition:** Emphasize the objectives of 1) gathering career-related insights and 2) making professional connections through the speaker.

- **Usefulness:** You might talk about the value of learning about individual career paths, experiences associated with different roles, and essential skills for those roles. The professional relationship established between the student and the practitioner has the potential to be highly influential should openings arise for an internship, entry level position, or another fruitful contact. In fact, most anthropologists find jobs through their professional networks. Advising students to keep in touch periodically with members of their network enables them to keep their contacts updated and signals that they continue to need help and advice. Stress that students should never leave an informational interview without asking, "Who else would be helpful for me to speak with?"

- **Key questions:** You could encourage the class to develop some questions on their own. Once all the questions have been shared, choose broad, general questions about the practitioner's career as well as advice questions. This ACRN tool on <u>Networking and Informational Interviews</u> offers examples.

- **Lesson:** Informational interviews can make career discovery and the job search process informative, interesting, and enjoyable.

Practicing

While rehearsing the questions can be completed as homework assignments, the final run-through and actual interview occur during class time.

- What tips can help students feel comfortable during informational interviews?

  - Have students work with a partner to learn about a past summer job
  - Require that they have their questions in front of them
  - Urge them to take notes to facilitate any follow-up questions
  - After practicing, record a few volunteers doing an informational interview so that they and the class can learn from their performance

- How can you improve your students' proficiency?

  - Set a goal of making the informational interview flow like an interesting conversation; watching a short video could be useful
  - Encourage students to connect to something the practitioner said when posing a new question
  - Focus on student nonverbals (e.g., good eye contact, expressions of interest) as an indicator of engagement
  - Expect students to obtain names/contact information of other possible practitioners
  - Require both verbal and email thank you notes, sharing what they learned and how it was helpful to them

- What are the key roles when the speaker visits the class?

  - Ask for a volunteer to serve as the lead, or MC, to:
    - Describe the goals: to learn about the speaker's career and advice for the class and how to conduct an informational interview
    - Call on class members to ask the questions
    - Keep track of time
    - Intervene when necessary to keep the interview on track

- o   If you have agreed on seven basic questions to ask the speaker, request seven class volunteers to pose them
  - o   Have remaining students develop additional questions, time permitting
  - o   Stress that note-taking is mandatory since it suggests interest, allows students to capture key insights, and serves as a memory aid
  - o   Conduct a dry run which includes scenarios where time is short and plentiful at the end so the class is prepared for both possibilities

- **Lesson:** Requiring the students to learn the technique and complete specific tasks before the visit demonstrates your confidence in their abilities.

The Technology

Any technology issues typically fall to the instructor or to the department's tech support. Test your equipment (e.g., projector, microphone, camera, internet speed) to ensure it is in good working order. This ACRN tool on <u>Professional Etiquette for In-Person and Remote Meetings</u> offers other suggestions.

The Informational Interview

Remind the students that this informational interview is *their* meeting—that is, it is their job to ensure it is as successful as possible. Ask for any last-minute questions or concerns. Make sure they have their laptops or notepads ready for taking notes. Tell them that you know they will do a great job. Then it is showtime!

- Since you sent the email, welcome the practitioner

- If the visit is virtual, check that everyone can see and hear each other

- Turn the event over to the MC and allow the event to unfold

- Follow the MC in thanking the speaker at the end

- **Lesson:** Balancing what the students learned in terms of both content and process helps them to understand the informational interview holistically.

The Debrief and Thank You

Reflecting and discussing the outcomes of the visit offer the students opportunities to learn from each other.

- Ask the students questions about the insights they gained:

    o **Content:** What were some key points you learned from the speaker?
      - What surprised you the most about what the speaker said?
      - To what extent did the speaker's advice resonate with you?
    o **Process:** What worked well about the event?
      - How well did we work together?
      - What should be done differently with future speakers?

- Now ask the speaker to offer input on the informational interview and any advice on doing these interviews in the future.

- After the speaker leaves, request two volunteers to write a thank you email, choosing from those who did not play a prominent role in the speaker's visit

- Offer any suggested edits to the email and then send it on behalf of the class

- **Lesson:** Soliciting student feedback on their performance helps solidify this technique in their minds.

Documenting the Connection

One important documentary source, LinkedIn, allows students to post their professional profiles, and connect with and message others. Yet, when learning how to develop a professional network or capture specific information about careers, it is useful to supplement LinkedIn with notes. Have the class create their own spreadsheets with the following:

- Name and contact information
- Date of informational interview
- Summary of career discussion
- Career advice
- Referrals
- Any follow-up
- Written thank you sent

26. Teaching with Blogposts

Priscilla Rachun Linn

A blogpost is a piece of writing, published on a blog (short for weblog), where people can share their ideas, perspectives, and information. Teaching students how to create engaging and informative blogposts helps develop clear thinking, a chain of logic, and succinct writing skills. Opportunities to integrate blogposts into coursework range from highlighting the value of specific course themes, to describing a field or lab experience, to elucidating key research results. Proficiency in writing blogposts is easily transferable to the workplace in the form of summarized content, impactful communications, and reader-friendly reports.

Why should students be able to write a blogpost?

Blog writing is excellent practice for:

- Organizing your thoughts
- Defining a major point and supporting it
- Writing in a clear, condensed manner
- Maintaining a tone and a voice
- Discovering which examples help corroborate an argument
- Understanding how to accept and learn from an editor's changes
- Creating emails, memos, and reports that co-workers will read and respect

How can instructors help students acquire the skills for creating a blogpost?

Teach how to identify key points for a successful blog by:

- Reading well-written blogposts and analyzing how the arguments flow together
- Knowing the story and thinking of it as writing a persuasive letter to a friend
- Expressing the blogpost from a personal point of view—not passive voice or stilted Artificial Intelligence

- Using the first paragraph to introduce the topic, experience, or opinion and provide credentials for writing about it
- Listing the statements in order of importance which support the central topic, experience, or opinion
- Creating a diagram to chart the main point and substantiating text, if helpful
- Encouraging contact with the blog editor to answer questions
- Preparing students to accept edits
- Focusing on clear and concise statements and avoiding run-on sentences
- Excluding distracting and evaluative descriptors, particularly ones like "very" or "great"
- Eliminating phrases like "in my opinion," or "I would like to point out that," which add extra verbiage
- Running spell check and grammar check

What are the best strategies to grab an audience's attention immediately?

Engage readers by:

- Examining a variety of blogpost openings
- Challenging the reader, perhaps with a counterfactual or "what if" statement
- Putting forth an astounding number or statistic for further discussion
- Selecting a small detail or example to make the greater point
- Saying something unusual and/or honest about yourself
- Keeping the opening short and punchy
- Avoiding long, run-on sentences
- Knowing if it does not grab you, it will certainly not grab readers

How can an instructor help students create a captivating title?

Identify catchy language by:

- Finding good titles to emulate
- Looking at popular language in ads, on social media, or other media
- Provoking or slightly teasing the reader while maintaining respect
- Seeking sympathy from the reader

- Making the title relevant to current "slangy" language while not sounding unprofessional
- Again, knowing if the title does not grab you, it will not grab readers

How can a blogpost sound authoritative?

Provide specific examples for:

- Verifying the major point or argument
- Citing important authorities in the field, but not in a dry, academic voice
- Demonstrating expertise in the field with facts and on-the-ground observations
- Sounding professional and logical, not biased

Can you disregard length considerations?

Investigate length considerations by:

- Comparing the length of other blogposts in a collection to see the pertinence of their length
- Knowing that blogposts typically deliver concise, memorable, honed messages
- Working with editors to meet length requirements
- Realizing that lengthy blogs often contain excess, redundant, or irrelevant verbiage
- Understanding that many readers will not read a long blog

What role does the audience play?

Write for your audience by:

- Researching and writing for the audience who will read your blogpost

- Analyzing how other blogposts appeal to the blog's audience in commentaries

- Respecting the audience; knowing that many readers have limited time to read blogs

*ACRN's **<u>World of Work blog</u>** should be your first stop for blogposts to use in teaching!*

Below are some selected *World of Work* blogposts:

- <u>Why is it relatively straightforward and useful to incorporate practice into anthropology courses?</u>
- <u>Which tools have been relevant in my journey as an anthropologist delving into UX Research?</u>
- <u>How can storytelling unlock the world of anthropology?</u>
- <u>What can the new workbook, Career Tools for Anthropology, do for me?</u>

Interested in writing for the *World of Work* blog? Submit at:

<u>https://anthrocareerready.net/updates/world-of-work-blog/submit-a-wow-blog/</u>

Other Recommended Posts:

- Matt Artz - <u>Best Anthropology Blogs</u>

Many bloggers now write on platforms like Substack, Medium, or even LinkedIn instead of maintaining a personal blog website. You can search for your favorite authors and subscribe or follow them to see their latest posts.

While some independent publishing platforms are free, others may charge a subscription fee to publish with their services. However, you may also be able to make money on these platforms by offering paid subscriptions to newsletters or access to exclusive or early content.

Independent Publishing Platform Examples

- <u>Medium</u>
- <u>Substack</u>
- <u>Ghost</u>
- <u>Patreon</u>

The market is a rapidly evolving like much of tech, so watch for new applications and platforms in the future.

27. Teaching with Op-Eds

Jeff Martin and Ed Liebow

In 1970, *The New York Times* invented the "op-ed" page (i.e., literally, opposite editorial page). Since then, op-ed pieces have become popular and powerful communication tools that are regular features of nearly every newspaper. Writing an op-ed combines a persuasive argument with concise storytelling. It is not a recitation of facts but rather a 600 to 800-word essay which hooks the reader, spells out the problem, and offers a solution of interest to policy makers and the general public. Newspapers accept unsolicited op-eds because they represent a diverse set of community viewpoints in contrast to the editorial board's perspective.

Teaching your students to take a position on an issue (local to global), make a concise and coherent case, and identify solutions will enable them to contribute to public policy issues that matter to them. What a great opportunity to apply their anthropological training within the wider community! And, your students gain from the experience, with benefits similar to those described in the ACRN tool <u>Teaching with Blogposts</u>.

What is a good checklist for crafting a compelling piece?

1. Study the Publication

Have your students read several articles to identify the following features:

- **Tone:** Is it formal, conversational, witty, or provocative?
- **Content focus:** Does it lean towards data, personal stories, or opinionated commentary?
- **Structure:** Does it prefer concise, punchy pieces or detailed, exploratory articles?
- **Vocabulary:** Does it use accessible language or assume specialized knowledge?
- **Word count:** What is the word limit for op-eds?

2. Know the Audience

- Impress upon your students the importance of tailoring their tone and content to a publication's readers which requires understanding the publication's audience, values, and editorial style.
- Share this science homecoming link (https://sciencehomecoming.com/) with your students, so that they can find local newspapers across the continental U.S.
- Assign the students to research the demographics (e.g., age, education level, occupation) and interests of the readers.
    - **Example:** A piece for *The New York Times* will differ in tone and complexity compared to one for a local community newsletter.
- Coach the students to consider the political, cultural, or social leanings of the audience.
    - **Example:** A business publication like *The Wall Street Journal* may favor data-driven arguments, while a lifestyle magazine like *Vogue* may prefer narrative-driven content.
- Encourage them to use simple, clear, and concise language while avoiding jargon (e.g., "hegemonic," "problematize") since they are writing for a broad, general audience. o For fun: Have them find out <u>which academic jargon best defines them</u>.

3. Start with a Strong "News" Hook

Help the students connect issues in which they are interested with something relevant that is happening in the current news cycle.

- Recommend students open with a striking fact, compelling anecdote, or provocative question to grab readers' attention immediately. Introducing a human element is a great way to start: how is the community or, better yet, an actual person being affected? In <u>a Common Dreams op-ed</u> regarding DACA (Deferred Action for Childhood Arrivals), Robin Valenzuela started this way:

In 2013, undocumented immigrant Alicia Chavez (not her real name) was arrested by Border Patrol and deported to Mexico, leaving her four American-born daughters with their father. Shortly after, Alicia received alarming news: her two youngest daughters, aged 10 and 12, had been abused by their father, and Child Protective Services had placed them with a foster family. Though Alicia fought to regain custody of her daughters from Mexico, her lack of money and resources presented insurmountable barriers; reluctantly, she forfeited her parental rights. Her daughters remained in the U.S. child welfare system.

- The openings the students write should set the stage for their arguments and entice readers to keep reading.

4. Define the Argument Clearly

Work with students to ensure their key idea is well formulated.

- Students should state their main argument early, usually in the first paragraph. In an op-ed in the *LA Times* regarding indoor heat standards, Nicholas Shapiro and Bharat Jayram Venkat wrote:

  A state board recently voted unanimously to create long-awaited indoor heat standards for California workers. After a final legal review, that will mean protections for millions of people with jobs in warehouses, kitchens and other workplaces that are getting dangerously hot as the climate warms. The board made one glaring exception, however — for prisons and jails.

- The argument of an op-ed differs from the argument of a traditional academic essay. The goal of an op-ed, as a persuasive or provocative writing form, is to present a clear and impactful viewpoint, often calling for action or a change in perspective. An academic essay is aimed at analyzing, exploring, or proving a thesis within a scholarly framework.

- In essence, an op-ed prioritizes immediacy, clarity, and persuasion, while an academic essay emphasizes depth, rigor, and critical analysis.

5. Structure the Argument

Coach your students to:

- Organize their op-eds around two or three key points that supports their thesis or perspective.
- Introduce each point in its own short paragraph with evidence or examples.

6. Use Evidence and Expertise

Confirmation from other sources will be an effective source of support for your students' viewpoints.

- It is essential for students to back up their claims with statistics, studies, or real-life examples.

- Highlighting their authority or unique perspective on the topic will serve them well. The earlier their viewpoint appears in the op-ed, the better (i.e., usually around paragraphs two and three). In an <u>op-ed in *The Guardian*</u> regarding the coaching change at the University of Alabama, Tracie Canada wrote:

  As someone who follows college football, I was shocked by the announcement. After almost two decades and six national championships in Tuscaloosa, Saban seemed a rock-solid fixture. But as an anthropologist and ethnographer who specializes in the intersection of race and sport, I was more concerned with what the news meant for the players, given how the timing of and secrecy surrounding these hires highlight a striking disconnect in football's focus on family.

- Recommend that your students avoid unnecessary repetition or overly complex explanations.

7. Engage Emotionally

Explain to your students that op-eds are typically written to produce an emotional impact on the reader.

- They use vivid language, personal stories, or rhetorical questions to make the argument resonate.
- Op-eds employ quotes from or stories about individuals to make the key points.
- Unlike anthropological research, op-eds appeal directly to values, empathy, or shared experiences to connect with readers.
- Hugh Gusterson, an anthropologist who has had op-eds published in many major news outlets, recommends replacing abstract nouns with visually evocative language:

  Soviet nuclear testing in Kazakhstan left in its wake serious medical issues becomes *Soviet nuclear testing in Kazakhstan left in its wake mothers nursing deformed babies and teens wasting away with leukemia.*

8. Take a position

Stipulate that an op-ed article reveals the writer's stand on an issue. Students will need to:

- Provide strong arguments about an issue in the news, avoiding the tendency to explain all sides of an issue (i.e., considered analysis). Editors are looking for timeliness, relevance, creative new ideas, or controversy.

- Use headlines strategically, a tactic that is especially powerful when transitioning to what readers can do. This <u>op-ed from the *Minneapolis Post*</u> worked quite effectively: Let's help Minnesota teachers hang on in 2022 and beyond.

- Conclude with a memorable closing that reiterates the thesis. In the <u>*NY Times* op-ed</u>, For Puerto Ricans, Another Reminder That We Are Second-Class Citizens, Yarimar Bonilla concluded with:

  As Justice Sonia Sotomayor argued in her dissenting opinion, access to health care and support for those with disabilities should not be a question of politics but, like self-determination, a matter of fundamental human rights.

9. Address Counterarguments

To strengthen students' credibility in writing op-eds, they will need to acknowledge and refute potential objections.

- Suggest that they present their arguments and recommendations first.
- Toward the end of the opinion essay, they can address the counterarguments.

10. Edit Ruthlessly

The goal is to eliminate unnecessary words and sharpen the points for impact. A smorgasbord of strategies is available to students:

- After writing a sentence, attempt to make it shorter.
- Write shorter paragraphs.
- Intentionally vary sentence length so that longer sentences are followed by short, punchy ones.
- Ask a peer for feedback.
- Read the piece aloud to catch awkward phrasing or unclear arguments.
- Edit when you are fresh.

How do you familiarize students with op-eds?

Introducing students to the op-ed writing format can occur in a variety of ways:

- Use some classroom time to teach op-ed writing basics, help students identify their issue, argument, and solutions, and review a draft of what they have written.
- Offer departmental workshops on writing effective op-ed articles.
- Introduce students to the op-ed format and then assign an op-ed article pertaining to the course content in lieu of a mid-term exam.
- Publicly recognize each student whose op-ed was selected for the student newspaper or local news outlet.

Final Tips

Getting an op-ed published is partly a numbers game and can be difficult, especially in major regional newspapers (e.g. *The San Francisco Chronicle, The Chicago Tribune, The Boston Globe*) unless you are nationally recognized on a hot-button topic. If your students are confident enough about their topics, encourage them to give it a try!

However, the odds of students getting something published increase greatly if they submit to a local publication. All the better if they are able to blend a national issue with a local angle. For example, congressional staff monitor local press stories to determine grassroots support or opposition to proposals.

Before your students pitch their work to a newspaper, make sure they read the op-ed submission guidelines. When their op-eds are accepted, it is a time to celebrate. If their op-eds are rejected, "try, try again."

Resources are available to help you send and gain acceptance for your op-ed, including the Op-Ed Project, Science Homecoming, and the Scholars Strategy Network.

Once the newspaper accepts your piece, work as cooperatively as you can with the paper's editors. Newspaper editors usually offer excellent suggestions. Disputing edits, unless they truly miss the point you are trying to make, delays publication of your piece and could make editors look dimly at your future submissions.

NOTE: A letter to the editor can also be an effective way to raise awareness about a topic already in the news. Keep it to just a paragraph or two.

References

1. The Op-Ed Project

2. Science Homecoming

3. The Scholars Strategy Network

4. Over the past 20 years, anthropologist Mark Mansperger (Washington State University) has published more than 45 op-eds in the local *Tri-City Herald*, on topics ranging from politics to economics to the environment.

Darby Stapp and Victoria Boozer, both with the *Journal of Northwest Anthropology*, interviewed him regarding his latest publication, *My Ideological Battle: Confronting Social Dogma with Anthropological Op-Eds*.

Read all about it in this *Anthropology News* piece: https://www.anthropology-news.org/articles/confronting-social-dogma-with-anthropological-op-eds-an-interview-with-mark-mansperger-darby-stapp-and-victoria-boozer/

28. Exploring Complex Issues with the Delphi Technique

Riall W. Nolan

Anthropologists recognize that when collecting data, it is important to know what the right questions are. With problems that are not well understood, ambiguous or unknown, it helps to get the "lay of the land" before making detailed plans or designing in-depth surveys. The Delphi Technique can help.

Delphi is *not* a sample survey. It is a qualitative technique which is relatively simple and quick. It is useful in exploring unknown territory, including topics with multiple facets or dimensions, or matters that are interdisciplinary in nature. Its insights and findings can help to define key characteristics, criteria, or issues, and to prioritize them so as to generate understanding to guide in-depth data gathering at a later time. By engaging a specific set of participants, the Delphi Technique helps investigators understand what is worth looking at in a situation, how various factors combine or come together, and specifically, where more data might be needed.

Some Uses for the Delphi Technique:

- Goal setting
- Listing problems
- Needs assessments
- Evaluating alternative proposals
- Developing alternatives
- Mapping differences of opinion
- Canvassing expert opinion
- Identifying the most salient information on a topic

Process

Delphi works best with a relatively small group of carefully selected respondents. The technique is iterative, involving several rounds of highly focused questioning, each round building on the answers from the last.

Delphi surveys are typically not long, and usually consist of only a few carefully worded queries. The initial question or issue is carefully framed, together with a set of initial requests for input. The question and requests are sent to a pre-selected list of people, who are asked to provide written, detailed feedback on the problem and/or the issues identified.

The results of this first round are summarized, analyzed, and used to help structure the second round. In the second round, more detailed questions may be asked. More focused questions (for example, oriented to an issue which has been raised in the first round) may be asked.

The second round can be used to help structure a third round, if necessary. Three rounds are usually the maximum.

The technique does not guarantee that a consensus will emerge, or that the problem will be completely understood. However, it usually succeeds in illuminating the scope and significance of the issue, together with some salient examples.

Getting Started

Delphi begins with an initial questionnaire and an identified group of 10-40 respondents, each of whom is assumed to be reasonably knowledgeable about some aspect(s) of the topic under investigation.

The questionnaire should be short, concise, and concrete, stating the problem, any necessary rules or assumptions, and the questions you would like them to address. You should ask for responses at the level of generalization that will be most useful to you.

Each respondent answers the questionnaire in writing, and the results are reviewed. This review generates a summary of what is known about the issue, and will bring up additional questions.

These new questions are put into a second questionnaire—perhaps in the form of ideas, issues, or alternatives.

For example:

- If you did not get enough suggestions, ask for more
- If some suggestions look promising, ask for more details
- If all the suggestions look feasible, ask people to rank them.

Respondents are then asked to comment, often by ranking or evaluating the results from the first round. The process continues until the researchers are satisfied.

How ACRN Has Used Delphi

ACRN used the Delphi technique when we were trying to understand how practitioners assessed the academic training they had received. We selected a group of about 40 younger practitioners, and asked them two questions in our initial round:

- What did you *not* get taught in school which would have helped you **GET** your job?

- What were you *not* taught in school which would have helped you **DO** your job?

After collating and analyzing their responses, we sent out a second-round questionnaire. It focused on two areas of their initial responses: methods and communicating anthropology to others. The key results are illustrated in this article[1].

An Example You Can Use

Problem:

Ethics is a major concern in the training of anthropologists, but relatively little is known about the ethical issues faced by practitioners. Designing a course in "The Ethics of Practice" would require quite a bit of new information about what these ethical issues are and how practitioners deal with them. Delphi could be used to elicit this information, thus forming the basis for a focused and relevant course design.

Procedure:

Begin by drafting a short but clear statement of the purpose and rationale for the Delphi survey. Then select respondents (10-40) who are younger practitioners on the job for, say, three years or more. These people could be your own alumni or come from other programs. Try to get variety in terms of the jobs they do and the sectors in which they work.

Contact them, explain the survey, and ask if they are willing to participate. Send them Round One questions. Collect their answers, analyze them, and construct Round Two questions based on their responses. After analyzing these responses, decide if you want or need to do a Round Three.

Rounds Two and Three do not necessarily have to include all the original respondents, but might instead involve a subset, focusing on one or more specific issues identified by some of them in Round One.

Problem — **Lack of information about ethical issues in practice**

Round Questions:

- Have you observed ethical issues, problems, or situations at work?
- Can you describe (without details) what sorts of issues these are?
- Can you describe whether they are resolved, and if so, how?
- Can you describe (without details) your role, if any, in resolution?
- Can you describe how well your academic training prepared you to do this?

Round Questions:

- Round One responses revealed a range of issues, many of which fell into the following categories: (list them here). Can you rank these in terms of how serious they are?
- If you have been involved in helping to resolve any of them, can you describe the kinds of things you needed to know to be effective?
- Can you describe specific things that might be included in academic training programs to prepare practitioners to deal with ethical issues?

Round Questions:

- As a final question, can you list (using bullet points) some of the major characteristics of ethical issues in the workplace that students should be made aware of?

Reference

1. Nolan, Riall W. and Elizabeth K. Briody. 2024, "How career ready are your students? Reflections on what we are (not) teaching anthropology students," *Annals of Anthropological Practice*, 48(1): 5-19, May.

29. Creating Learning Contracts for Student Growth

Riall W. Nolan

Often in a course or a program, there is insufficient time to cover all possible aspects of a topic. Sometimes you have individual students with very specific needs and interests not covered in the regular department curriculum. Learning contracts are an easy and effective way to deal with this issue. A learning contract is a professional development plan for self-directed learning in specific areas not fully covered by your program. It is an effective way of extending student skills and knowledge.

As students move through your program, they may identify areas of knowledge they consider important in their training or their interests may develop in directions not fully covered by the curriculum. Indeed, some of what they may wind up looking for may not be contained in a typical anthropology program at all, such as knowledge about human geography, decision science, organizational dynamics, business strategy, economics, or Geographic Information System (GIS). Learning contracts are one way of filling in important blanks.

Learning contracts help students learn by themselves, outside your formal and official program. The learning contract model described here is based on models developed years ago by educator Malcolm Knowles[1,2]. They can be adapted to a wide variety of topics and situations.

Concept

The concept of learning contracts is not new. At most universities, students have the option to engage in "independent study" of one sort or another. Such opportunities are usually structured to fit within the standard academic calendar and are closely supervised by one or more instructors.

Yet not all students have experience with independent study, and not all programs have room within them for these opportunities. Learning contracts, as described here, are a form of independent study, but more flexible and more under the control of the student.

Although you can certainly make learning contracts fit within your existing program, they can easily run independent of these restrictions. A learning contract puts the student, rather than the instructor, in charge of what is learned and how. A learning contract might never appear on a student's academic record. And although the student may draw on university resources (e.g., libraries, databases) for some of their learning, outside resources and experiences may prove even more useful.

Setting Up a Learning Contract

A learning contract of this type asks an individual student to define what they want to learn and why. It then asks them to specify how they will learn what they plan to learn, and most importantly, how they will know when they have been successful.

A typical learning contract asks a student to describe the following:

- **Learning objectives**: What do you want to learn and why? What have you learned so far? What is missing? Where do you want to take your learning next? Express this in a set of clear learning objectives—statements which are concrete, measurable, and specific.
- **Strategies and resources**: How will you accomplish your learning objectives? Some resources are available at your university, some available outside. They include people, materials (e.g., books and tapes), activities, and environments. The contract should describe what you will do to learn, how you will acquire this knowledge, and when you will begin and end this process.
- **Outputs**: What will you produce to show you are learning? Describe, specifically and in detail, the results, products or outcomes of your learning. Examples of typical products include reports, essays, presentations, designs, collections, and demonstrations.
- **Assessment criteria**: How will these products be judged? What standards will be applied? Will you alone be the judge, or will it involve others?

Instructor Input

Although a learning contract can be used independent of an academic program, some instructor input is both necessary and desirable. Explaining how learning contracts work to students has several positive outcomes. They offer students an additional learning option, permit more flexibility within the program, and help students develop their skills as independent learners. As an instructor, you can decide how much involvement, if any, you want to have.

An Example of a Learning Contract

Let's see how learning contracts might work in practice. Halfway through their graduate program, a student decides that they would really like to work internationally and with different groups of people. They might describe their objective this way:

I want to learn more about cross-cultural group leadership. I have been in groups before containing people from different cultures. It isn't always easy to get things done, because people have different cultural styles. Since I want to work overseas, I want to learn as much as I can about how to work with, and eventually manage, multicultural groups.

Here is one example of a learning contract that might be developed from this objective:

Learning objectives	Resources and strategies	Outputs	Assessment
• Identify characteristics of effective cross-cultural groups. • Examine conflict resolution strategies which can be used successfully in a cross-cultural group setting. • Analyze what key writers and practitioners see as the skills required for successful cross-cultural group leadership. • Gain experience in working with and managing a cross-cultural group in a situation where the potential for group conflict exists.	• Conduct a library search, reading relevant literature. • Interview key professionals. • Collect own material. • Listen to podcasts. • Take relevant courses. • Secure an internship with a cross-cultural group, preferably overseas. • Attend conferences and workshops.	• A summary article, 2,500 words long, which reviews salient literature, analyzes the nature of cross-cultural work groups, and discusses strategies for conflict resolution in diverse groups. • A training syllabus for a two-day workshop for people intending to work in cross-cultural situations. • Tape-recorded interviews with group facilitators. • A videotape of a session in which the student applies cross-cultural mediation and conflict resolution techniques.	• Article is published in either one of the academic journals dealing with cross-cultural issues or in one of the NGO newsletters. • A training workshop is developed and presented, with evaluations of it. • Interviews conducted and videotapes are reviewed by the advisor and one other professor, with their written comments provided. • A written evaluation of the student's overseas internship is placed in student's file.

<h2 style="text-align:center">Sharing the Learning Contract with Others</h2>

Although the learning contract is centered on an individual student, it can be a negotiated document between you and one or more students. It can also be discussed and negotiated with selected others who are instrumental in student learning (e.g., other instructors, advisors, colleagues, supervisors, mentors, members of the student's network).

Your input and opinions—and those of others—can become particularly important at certain points in the planning process. For example, student learning needs are highly personal and should mainly reflect their own thinking. Learning activities, on the other hand, usually involve others. And the assessment of student learning outputs might, under some circumstances, be done best by other people (e.g., you, editors, mentors). However, throughout the process, the student is in charge.

Note that the range of resources and activities available to students for meeting their learning needs is considerable, both on and off campus. A professional development plan does not compete with—and certainly does not conflict with—your established academic program. Rather, it complements and extends student learning in specific ways, along lines that they themselves decide, based on their emerging professional interests and aspirations.

References

1. Knowles, M. S. 1984. *Andragogy in Action. Applying Modern Principles of Adult Education.* San Francisco, CA: Jossey Bass.

2. Knowles, M. S. 1986. *Using Learning Contracts: Practical Approaches to Individualizing and Structuring Learning.* San Francisco, CA: Jossey Bass.

30. Fostering Alumni & Student Connections on LinkedIn

Andrew Walsh

The best time to start a LinkedIn group for your students and alumni is 10 years ago. The second best time is **now**.

What do your students do after they graduate? Where in the world do they end up? How have they applied what they learned while studying anthropology with you?

Not only are these questions asked by a growing chorus of students, parents, reviewers, administrators, and others, they are questions anthropology instructors may be asking themselves. Often instructors have lost track of all but a few former students who pop up occasionally to request letters of reference. Some alumni are not as hard to track down as you might imagine. Many are already on LinkedIn – which bills itself as "the world's largest professional network" – just waiting to be found.

Forming a Current Student & Alumni LinkedIn Group

1. **Create a LinkedIn profile for yourself and then create a LinkedIn group.** When choosing a name, go with something broad enough to indicate that the group is open to current and former students as well as faculty and staff – something like "X University Anthropology Network". The more colleagues you can get involved, the more likely you are to attract current students and alumni who will seek out instructors they know/knew best.

2. **Find your alumni.**

   Search out your institution's LinkedIn page, click on "Alumni", and then search "anthropology" or any other terms that students might use to describe their degree or program. First you must "connect" with the alumni you find and then you can invite them to join your group. Again, asking colleagues to seek out and make connections of their own should help grow the network quickly. Former students are typically happy to be remembered and contacted in this way. They may have good things to say about the relevance of their anthropological training, are eager to visit classes as a guest speaker, and are willing to take on the role of mentor to those following in their footsteps.

3. **Get today's students to join your group since they are tomorrow's alumni.** It is easier to do this now than trying to track them down later. That in mind, invite your current students to create LinkedIn profiles; this ACRN tool can help. Either have them join your group or ask them to send you their profile names so you can invite them. Your institution's careers office might offer workshops on this. If students seem dubious or reluctant, it might help to incorporate this activity into their coursework. LinkedIn is a fascinating world to explore from an anthropological perspective, offering plenty of fodder for discussions and assignments.

   You might, for example, have your students explore LinkedIn while reading Ilana Gershon's excellent ethnography of job-seeking, _Down and Out in the New Economy_ (which includes a chapter on LinkedIn), and then lead a discussion of the complexities, potential, and limitations of the social relations enabled by the platform. In the end, students will learn that LinkedIn is not just for business students (a common misconception). In fact, it can be an excellent source of news and opportunities for those intent on work in <u>NGOs</u>, <u>UX (User Experience)</u>, or any number of <u>other fields</u>.

Now that you have a LinkedIn group, what can you do with it?

- Use it to connect with alumni who might be willing to talk with current students about their career paths, how they use their anthropological training in their current work, and what they wish they had known before graduating.

- Use it to connect current students who have certain career paths in mind with alumni who have already followed these paths. Rather than have current students contact alumni themselves, you might mediate and suggest they get together for a one-on-one "<u>coffee chat</u>", a common form of interaction among the platform's users.

- Use it to invite alumni to campus to participate in career panels, a career day (or evening), or an advisory group to departmental leadership about career readiness and changes in the workplace and technology.

- Use it to learn what alumni are doing ahead of program or departmental reviews in which you will be expected to report on the career trajectories of graduates.

- Use it to keep alumni who are working outside of anthropology connected to the discipline <u>by posting</u> news from the field and invitations to upcoming events on your group page.

- Use it to celebrate current and former students by publicly commenting on the accomplishments, milestones, or new positions they post on their own timelines.

- Use it to attest to the expertise of current and former students by <u>endorsing their skills</u> or contributing <u>recommendations</u> to their profiles. These affirmations double as opportunities to communicate the value of the distinctive skills and perspectives taught in anthropology programs.

For more ACRN resources concerning LinkedIn, see:

<u>LinkedIn Profile Checklist: 12 Sections to Make Your Profile Stand Out</u>

<u>Virtual Experience: What is it? How Do You Put It on Your Resume?</u>

31. Making Connections with Local Organizations

Laurie Schwede and Elizabeth K. Briody

Demonstrating the value and relevance of anthropology to your students and to those out in the world is essential to the teaching role. Identifying work opportunities can help expose students to workplace options as they begin planning their future. Students benefit from applying their anthropological toolkit across a range of projects, internships, and job opportunities. Similarly, organizations such as government agencies, companies, and nonprofits gain from the concepts and methods anthropology students can bring to current workforce and supply chain issues. Instructors can be the catalysts in connecting the classroom to the workplace. This tool offers suggestions on how to engage in organizational outreach and sustain connections once they are established.

Benefits to You and Your Students

Figuring out the nearby organizational landscape is the first step in building connections between you and employers. With such relationships, you will be positioned to propose:

- a client-based class project
- job shadowing
- a service-learning experience
- an internship for one or more of your students

If you maintain your relationships over time, your students will benefit from employer career advice as well as:

- access to professional networks
- mentoring
- possible job referrals
- references

Benefits to Local Organizations

Partnering with a nearby university is desirable because of value adds:

- extension of professional networks, strengthening the connections between "town and gown"
- conduit for research possibilities
- inexpensive source of student input with advisor
- an anthropological perspective on organizational issues
- possibility of a job pipeline
- enhancement of organizational reputation
- opportunity to "give back" to the community

How Do You Begin?

Numerous options for exploring your ecosystem are open to you. Although much of the work involves exploration, at some point you will be engaged in outreach and discussions with nearby organizational leaders. Consequently, you will need to practice your "pitch" to these leaders. Incorporating the benefits to them into the pitch will enable you to be most effective in this spearheading role.

1. Tap the Experts: Staff, Alumni, and Colleagues

- Contact your campus Career Planning Office to inquire about local employers with whom that office works

    - Find out the kinds of organizations where students intern each semester or summer
    - Indicate anthropology student interest in benefiting from local work experience
    - Ask about arranging introductory conversations with one or more employers

- Alumni from your Department

    - Create a LinkedIn Group of your current students, staff, and instructors with any known alumni; consider using this tool, <u>Fostering Alumni & Student Connections on LinkedIn</u>

- Reach out to any known alumni to participate in various departmental events (e.g., career panels, guest lectures, departmental workshops)
    - To connect with alumni, see our tool <u>Building Department-Alumni Connections</u>
  - Build relationships with those alumni who seem to have the capacity and interest in supporting student career readiness; arrange virtual and in-person meet-and-greets with selected students and faculty

- Colleagues from your Department or College

  - Learn which instructors have local organizational contacts and whether students are engaged with them and in what way
  - Brainstorm possible student projects with one or more of these contacts
  - Set up meetings with these contacts to probe their interest in working with you/your colleagues and your students

- Reach out to any research parks or business incubators associated with the university

  - To learn about the work occurring there, set up opportunities for students to use their observation and interviewing skills through facility tours and guest speakers, respectively
  - Interview university liaisons in these enterprises about project-related issues with which students might assist (e.g., class projects)

2. Brainstorm and Validate by Category

- Conceptualize organizations in three broad categories: business, nonprofits, and government

- Brainstorm local organizations that fit into those categories

  - Be aware that a medical organization like a hospital could be categorized as a private, nonprofit, or government entity
  - Recognize that some organizations may have multiple divisions, departments, or specialties, with multiple contacts that may offer opportunities

- Gather additional insights using the internet

  - **For Businesses:** Explore local business directories, largest employers, Fortune 500 companies, and companies headquartered in your city

- o **For Nonprofits:** Search for nonprofits and charities, nonprofit associations, foundations, museums, biggest nonprofits, most successful nonprofits and nonprofits and community groups in your city
  - o **For Government:** Examine your city (and/or county) government and programs, public services and government, federal executive boards, mayor's office, city council, city commissions, and city departments in your city

3. Treat Your Investigation as On-site Fieldwork

- Conduct a quick survey by driving around and recording the names of area organizations from visible signage

- Consult with knowledgeable professionals including reference librarians, the Chamber of Commerce, service organizations (e.g., Lions Club, Rotary International), United Way and others

- Network with community and university members to identify potential organizational options for student work experiences

4. Ask Students to Identify their Workplace Preferences

- Have students name local organizations corresponding to a list of work sectors where anthropologists work; consider using the organizations listed in the tool, <u>What can you do with a degree in anthropology?</u>

- Encourage students to think about an issue or domain of work that appeals to them such as domestic violence shelters, user experience, local tourism, courts, patient safety, research organizations, housing affordability, historic preservation, or organizational change; use the internet to develop lists of organizations for each issue or domain

- Have students identify whether these work sectors have at least one local match

- Assign students to do a "deep dive" into the websites of those local organizations of greatest interest to the students

<h1 style="text-align:center">Who Gets Involved?</h1>

- **For a Client-based Class Project:** An individual instructor would reach out to contacts at one or more area organizations to gauge their interest in sponsoring a class project

    - Focus on a problem or issue the client is facing; see our tool, <u>How do you set up a client-based project?</u> for examples
    - Ensure the scope is relatively narrow since the project concludes by the end of the term
    - Design the class project to be an integral part of the course

- **For Internships and Job Shadowing:**

    - An individual instructor or staff coordinator, often working collaboratively with the campus Career Planning Office, would investigate potential options for students; see our tool, <u>Setting Up an Internship Program</u>.
    - A student may also take the lead in exploring internship and job shadowing options

- **For Service Learning:** These experiences are usually the purview of the instructor that decides to integrate coursework with community service

It is always helpful to begin with some contacts. Your campus Career Planning Office should be able to advise you on working with local organizations and may be able to assist you with recommendations for specific organizations. You will learn about their processes for working with organizations and students.

If you are working on your own without the benefit of any knowledge of local organizations, start small. Reach out to one or two organizations and establish a connection with them. After your first collaboration, you will be able to learn from the experience and then consider whether you will try to resume, expand, or discontinue the relationship.

<h2 style="text-align:center">Tips for Maintaining the Organizational Relationship</h2>

Some time and energy will be necessary to sustain the relationship.

- Set up a meeting with the organization to provide and receive feedback; this <u>Post-Internship Evaluation Guide</u> may be useful

- If you/your students gained from the experience, ask your organizational contact about 1) considering a new project, service-learning opportunity, or intern/internship, 2) introducing you to a new contact elsewhere in the organization

- Invite your organizational contact(s) to participate in a department-sponsored event (e.g., panel discussion, social occasion, recognition ceremony)

- Explore your organizational contact's interest in offering career advice to your students, opportunities to expand their professional networks, or mentoring them

To allow the relationship to flourish indefinitely into the long-term, regardless of career moves, retirements, and the like:

- Find other departmental or university colleagues to partner with you

- Make as many contacts in the organization as possible

- Involve your students in more than one part of the organization

32. How Do You Set up a Client-based Class Project?

Susan Squires and Elizabeth K. Briody

Why do it?

- Students get "hands-on" experience working on a current problem for a "real" client, using their research, project management, communication, and collaboration skills.
- A creative thinking-learning experience is foundational as students transition to the workplace.
- To get hired, employers expect graduates to have some work experience which a class project offers.

Who participates?

- Junior and Senior level undergraduates
- Graduate students

How long is it?

- One semester

How do you find a client?

- Recruit clients through anthropologists in industry, non-profits, and government
- Tap into your own network
- Use the Career Readiness Commission network

Ethnographic Research Example

Best for Graduate Level or Advanced Undergraduate Classes

Goals

- Involve students in a "real-world" problem through project-based learning
- Develop skills through the direct application of ethnographic methods
- Build and extend theory based on analysis
- Work as a team to write and get input on a proposal, plan and conduct the research, and develop and deliver a final presentation to the client

Readings

- Assigned to parallel each project phase
- Types include the anthropological perspective, culture concept, comparisons of theoretical models, practical articles on creating field guides and coding methods, and theories on team building

Outcomes

- Research skill development, including supporting findings with theory or generating new theory
- Experience in project planning and execution

Search and Summary Example

Best for Undergraduate Level Classes

Goals

- Compile cases showing range of successful solutions anthropologists have developed in industry, non-profits, and government
- Provide short, bulleted case summaries
  - Problem
  - Approach
  - Outcome/Practical Significance
- Suggest ways to organize summaries

Outcomes

- Electronic and library search skills
- Clear, concise written summaries
- Creative options for organizing summaries
- Acquisition of lessons in problem solving

Blog Posts Example

Works with any level class

Goals

- Identify the knowledge, skills, and experiences from anthropology that helped prepare you for your career
- Describe near-term or medium-term career goals
- Offer advice to anthropology programs to improve student career readiness

Outcomes

- Reflection on anthropology's usefulness and relevance
- Written blog post to include in portfolio

For more detailed examples of each class project type, visit:

https://anthrocareerready.net/for-instructors/class-projects/

33. Client Engagement Best Practices

Ken C. Erickson and Elizabeth K. Briody

Working successfully with a client is based on factors such as appropriate expertise, adeptness in relationship building, identifying and responding to client interests and concerns, and quality and timeliness in the delivery of a product (e.g., research, program, process). A client is someone for whom you provide the needed services (e.g., research, advising, evaluation, program design) to assist with a problem, usually for a fee. A class project may also be designed around the client's problem.

Client Engagement Phases

This tool introduces a model of the key phases of client engagement. It offers advice on interacting with clients whether you are supervising a client-based class project, launching your own consulting practice, seeking new clients as a seasoned consultant, or working with senior leadership in your own organization. While all phases of the work matter, significant energy is required during the proposal stage to ensure you and the client share a common understanding of what the work will entail.

Phase 1: Discovery and Connection

How do I find a potential client?

Use the resources close at hand—including your own network among colleagues and friends—to expand your connections. (See the ACRN tool <u>Making Connections with Local Organizations</u>.)

- Enlist members of your network to offer you an entrée to organizations where they have relationships.

- Collaborate on a project with someone who already has an organizational client.

As you meet these new contacts, conduct informational interviews with them to learn about their organizations and the issues they face.

Other options to consider:

- Attend networking events, including local ones, to spread the word that you offer consulting services.

- Consider trade magazines and trade organizations to identify contacts.

- LinkedIn and other social media platforms may be a source of events and connections.

- Plan to attend area conferences, including those beyond anthropology.

- Respond to Requests for Proposals (RFPs) from local, state, or national organizations and government agencies.

Do not fear the cold call (i.e., calling an organization that does not know you) but do not rely on the cold call alone.

An essential part of networking involves marketing your services. Use these aids to assist:

- Create business cards and brochures of your services.

- Launch a website.

- Advertise on social media and in local news outlets.

Phase 2: Relationship Building

How do I establish a relationship with a client?

The phone and the internet are fine first steps, but there is power in meeting. A virtual or face-to-face meeting with a prospective client signals your interest in and commitment to a future relationship. If in person, try for a coffee or lunch meeting. The ritual of sharing a cup of coffee or a meal will allow you to learn about each other.

Luck favors the well prepared. Prepare for a first meeting by:

- Researching the organization

- Learning about the person you will meet.

Develop some opening thought-starter questions, such as:

- What are your primary responsibilities?

- How long have you been in that role?

What is keeping this client "awake at night?"

Strive to learn as much as you can about the client in your initial conversations—whether by phone, online, or in person. Clients always face an array of problems. Ultimately, you want to identify the nature of their work issue, organizational concern, or business predicament. If not intrusive when you meet in person, have a notebook handy to jot down key terms or insights. The notebook may also contain questions that you (or your team or students) have about the client and the organization.

Think of your first meeting as an initial semi-structured ethnographic interview. That's a skill you already have! You may wish to offer some suggestions on anthropological approaches to their concerns, thereby beginning to help your client from the "get-go," giving the client the sense that your first visit was time well-spent.

Avoid any discussion about politics or religion unless it is relevant to the client and their mission. After you have a contract and trust is built up, you can share personal concerns of common interest selectively.

Phase 3: Proposal and Negotiation

What do you cover in a proposal?

Let's say that the client is interested in having you work on a project. In most cases, they will ask you for a project proposal or Statement of Work (SOW). At a minimum, this document includes:

- Your approach to the client's problem

- How you plan to do the work

- Who will be involved

- When you expect the project to be completed

- How much the project will cost.

When the work is pro bono, you may not be asked for a formal proposal. However, it can be useful to develop a written proposal to ensure that you and the client are aligned on the stated problem and the work involved.

Have prior organizational actions been successful?

It is always helpful to have access to background material on the issue the client has raised:

- Has any prior research been done by or for the client?

- Are there organizational documents that might offer additional information?

Prior work (e.g., consultant report, employee turnover statistics) may prove fruitful in illuminating aspects of the context as well as the specific issue. If the client offers you any documentation, you are likely to be asked to sign a non-disclosure agreement (NDA).

What is the project deliverable?

Will you deliver a slide deck, video, other digital media, or a prose report? If done appropriately, a slide deck is often the preferred format for sharing your results (i.e., "deliverable"). Think of a Canva or PowerPoint slide deck as a handout that is designed to capture salient features of your work simply and concisely. When done well, someone who did not attend the presentation can absorb the vital insights and recommendations from your slide deck. Make sure you and your client are in agreement on how many times you or your team will make a final presentation.

Prose reports offer greater detail than a slide deck but they generally do not work well with clients who want to understand what you have learned quickly and effectively. If a narrative report is one of your deliverables, include an "Executive Summary" at the beginning. It may be the only part of your report that is widely read. Ultimately, the form of your deliverable will depend on your client's need to garner buy-in for your project's findings and recommendations.

Video and audio present both technical and communication challenges. Video involves time and costs to collect and edit. If you use video or audio, introduce your insights first. You want to avoid a situation in which the client focuses on extraneous details (e.g., participant's dress, accent, skin color) rather than what you intend for them to learn.

Is your client clear about your project plans and your ethical responsibilities?

Discuss and then document your approach and the nature, timing, and cost of your project's planned deliverables in the written agreement. This agreement should specify who owns the results, data, and the insights as well as specify your plans to maintain confidentiality and informed consent. It should be signed by you and the client. Large organizations may have their own contractual documents which require your signature.

Generally, "raw" data (e.g., interview transcripts, participant observation notes) are retained by the researcher. If your client wants access to this data, agree on how it may be used while still protecting confidentiality. Similarly, if you hope to present or publish non-proprietary findings, make clear that you will maintain organizational confidentiality unless your client prefers otherwise.

How will you handle course-corrections?

In exploratory research projects, early patterns may suggest the addition of new questions. Discussing the possibility of course-corrections will help avoid surprises. Your research plan should build in adequate time to reschedule or add interviews, or to include newly discovered contexts related to the problem being investigated.

Beware of "scope creep" in which the client seeks to append a new research direction to the original scope. The impact of this kind of redirection will compromise your time and budget. You may indicate that those new avenues for investigation are doable, but should occur in a Phase 2 of the project.

Do you know your cost and time commitment?

Your written project plan should be developed with a clear sense of your team's time and costs. In the case of a client-based class project, the course end-date dictates when the work must be concluded. Timeframes for other projects vary based on complexity, budget allocation, and other factors.

Figure the costs in staff time, equipment, and other expenses for each project step. Include your overhead such as fixed costs (e.g., internet, office), taxes, and a margin for profit. Pricing your work can be challenging. Consult with colleagues to find current practices regarding pricing within your field of practice.

At some point, you will need to discuss, and possibly negotiate, your project cost with your client. While recognizing the resources you will need to complete the project, acknowledge that your client likely faces constraints as well. Price reductions to meet client constraints should be reflected in reducing the project's scope or sample size to reach agreement on the budget.

Have you discussed how to manage travel?

Some anthropologists include travel as a lump sum component of their overall cost rather than providing unnecessary detail. Others submit receipts for travel directly to the client, separate from the proposal. State and federal guidelines online will help you estimate per-diem, travel, and lodging costs. Experienced consultants do not skimp on lodging and meals, given that fieldwork and travel require well-rested researchers. Some clients, especially government clients, may have their own travel reimbursement requirements to which you will have to respond and provide adequate documentation, such as itemized receipts.

Have you discussed payment processes?

For student projects, suggest that your client cover any student expenses (e.g., government rate for mileage) and/or expenses for participant incentives (e.g., gift cards).

Negotiate an up-front charge, often up to half the project cost, with the balance paid upon project completion. For many clients, interim and final payments occur at least 60 days after submission. However, learn your client's payment process. Some clients prefer invoicing and payment on a monthly basis which ensures that they are satisfied and you are paid for work provided.

Phase 4: Project and Client Management

Do you track your project's phases?

Creating a Gantt chart will enable you to follow the project's progress. This horizontal timeline portrays project phases arranged sequentially with weeks or days at the top of the chart, along with an indication of team members responsible for these phases. Providing an abbreviated chart in the proposal helps the client visualize your process.

As the project begins, set aside time for discussion with the client and their key stakeholders to get a broad understanding of the organizational context and some initial perspectives on the client's issue. Later, when interviews and other ethnographic methods are involved, it can be challenging to complete them in a timely way due to "busy" calendars. If you are doing organizational work, ask for the client's assistance in sending out an email to:

- Notify employees that the project is underway

- Seek their cooperation in responding to requests quickly.

Be sure to discuss the necessity of time needed for analysis. Many clients assume that once the data is collected, the project is about to wrap up. A good rule of thumb for you: one hour of data collection yields about five hours of analysis and presentation development.

Review your progress and inform the client of any roadblocks or changes to your timeframe. Track your budget against your Gantt chart.

When will you provide feedback on what you are learning?

Clients are eager to know the status of the project.

- Informal conversations offer an opportunity to provide some details.

- Formal updates, complete with preliminary slide decks, enhance the client relationship and offer assurance that the work is progressing.

Common project milestones often occur at the project's midpoint, or quarterly in the case of long projects. These updates should include early insights as well as planned actions for the next phase. They also provide a time set aside when both parties can focus on what is being learned, ask pertinent questions, and align perspectives. Dialog helps build and extend the relationship and will improve the reception of your final deliverable.

Will your client join you in fieldwork?

While not always part of a project, client participation in fieldwork can offer benefits:

- The client may come to understand the value of ethnographic work.

- They may enjoy the process enough to become a repeat client.

- They may come to a more intimate and actionable understanding of the problem at hand.

However, client participation must be managed carefully. Clients must be cautioned not to jump to unwarranted conclusions based on their partial participation in the work.

For student projects, a client may participate in several important ways:

- Spending time helping students understand the organization

- Offering further detail about the potential sources of the problem being investigated

- Reviewing pertinent policies and regulations.

In organizational work, clients would not be involved in interviews with organizational members for a number of reasons, including interviewee confidentiality. Prior discussion and setting clear expectations regarding client participation is key to working with clients in the field.

Phase 5: Project Delivery and Follow Up

Will your final report convey your work in a convincing and actionable way?

At least four strategies can help you address this question:

- Be responsive to client review/approval structures as you prepare to finalize your work.

- Share one or two insights with a few of your most interested and knowledgeable participants to gauge their reactions.

- Hold a preliminary review with a small client group to explain the key discoveries and gather perspectives on your proposed recommendations.

- Confirm attendees at the final presentation and ask about their expectations.

Do you know if the client found the work helpful?

A simple post-presentation evaluation, often done verbally, can offer important feedback. A few questions are sufficient, such as:

- How satisfied were you with this presentation?

- What would you have liked to hear less about?

- What would you have liked to learn more about?

Sometimes, clients may use your work to make organizational, marketing, or policy changes. Check with them sometime after the project has ended to find out whether any changes were implemented. You may discover they have taken actions that were helpful to the organization. Since organizations are unlikely to broadcast the impact of your work, find out! It may help you gain future clients.

Will others find your work helpful?

At the end of the project, ask the client if there might be other venues through which you might present non-proprietary aspects of your efforts. If possible, collect written recommendations to use in your marketing for future clients. Be ready to share your general, non-proprietary and methodological insights with others in your client's work sector, and with students, too.

34. Setting Up an Internship Program

Edward (Ted) Maclin

An **internship** is a short-term work experience that teaches skills to interns (typically students) while providing temporary assistance to organizations. An **internship program** is the set of policies and procedures that ensure these professional learning experiences offer meaningful, practical work related to a student's field of study or career interests. A successful internship program is a collaboration between the student interns, their university supervisors, and their organizational hosts.

Frequent communication among all three parties is key! The university supervisor, often an anthropology instructor or internship coordinator, can enhance the internship process and outcomes by checking in with the interns and host supervisors at least bi-weekly.

What are the benefits?

For the Interns:

- Gain exposure to the work world to discover their own interests, including employment features they appreciate as well as dislike
- Contribute to projects and tasks that offer hands-on work experience and benefits (e.g., conducting interviews, making presentations, writing reports)
- Use their existing skills in real-world situations as well as acquire new skills
  - While still relatively protected, interns can and should start to experience the pressure and accountability of real-world work; learn how to arrive at and defend their decisions; and understand the decision-making process used in their host organizations
- Learn to interact and collaborate with new colleagues
- Expand their professional networks (e.g., with other interns, seasoned leaders)
- Enter the larger community of working professional anthropologists
- Find it easier to land a future position in the same industry
- Gain confidence in their ideas and choices
- Learn how to fail and recover from making mistakes

For individual departments or the university as a whole:

- Offer workplace experience to students to enhance their academic learning
- Develop relationships with organizations in the wider community, strengthening their connections and reputation
- Launch students into the work world, thereby improving their job placement rate post-graduation
- Develop a reputation as a talent incubator

For the host organizations:

- Secure access to a source of temporary workers
- Observe, train, and assess these workers for their future potential
- Build a pipeline of new hires with a known university (or one or more of its programs)

How do internships differ between undergraduate and graduate students?

Question	Undergraduate Students	Graduate Students
Who participates in internships?	Typically students in their Junior or Senior Year	Students at any point during their degree
How long do internships last?	Usually one term; internship credit hours vary from one to three and may be repeated	Internship length varies but typically involves deeper interactions with host organizations
What is the time investment?	Often full time during the summer months and part time during the spring and fall	An internship may be part of a student's practicum or thesis work and last longer than a term
What do internships focus on?	May either be narrowly-focused, or broad but shallow, given the short time period and student's lack of prior experience	Generally build on previous experience

Can students get paid for their internship work and still earn credit?

Yes! Many internship programs allow students to get paid and earn university credit. Differences exist across programs, host organizations, and U.S. states:

- At some universities, students can earn internship credit for work they are already doing in their job—as long as they can define and meet specific goals relevant to anthropology
- Some nonprofit organizations may not have the budget to pay interns, though in some cases, anthropology departments may have funds available to support unpaid interns
- In some U.S. states, interns receiving academic credit may be unpaid; while in others if they are receiving academic credits, they must be paid at least minimum wage

Interns should never be solely free labor. Regardless of financial compensation, internship value related to student learning, skill-building, and networking must be clearly evident.

How do students get credit?

In the short term, an instructor may be able to supervise internships through a "directed research" course. From a longer-term perspective, an instructor may develop a dedicated course such as:

ANTH 4970 INTERNSHIP at the University of Memphis

The ANTH 4970 Individual Directed Internship in Anthropology is available for 1-3 course credit hours which can be applied to the major or minor (no more than 3 credit hours can apply to the major or minor). Typically, each credit hour requires 50 hours of internship work (i.e., 3 credit hours requires 150 hours of internship work). Internship goals are: (1) To offer the student practical, professional knowledge and experience relevant to the discipline of anthropology; (2) To provide the host agency with valuable assistance in the achievement of a specific objective or product. The Internship may be focused on any area relevant to the discipline of Anthropology. Each internship is to be defined and agreed upon by the student, the host agency internship supervisor, and the Anthropology faculty member who agrees to supervise the internship and serve as instructor of record.

An established campus career center may facilitate approval of credit through coordination between the department and host organization.

On the University side, who oversees interns?

Anthropology Department

- Some departments have an internship coordinator
- Undergraduate interns may be the responsibility of the undergraduate advisor while graduate students report to their committee chairs
- Alumni relationships with the department often lead to the establishment of an internship pipeline for successive student cohorts

Individual Instructor

- Students enroll in an organized class for their internships
- Instructors may offer courses with internship options embedded in them
- Students may approach instructors based on common affinities, with internships functioning like directed reading courses and course credits based on hours worked
- Instructors may be able to negotiate extra compensation or course reductions to supervise interns

University Internship or Career Center

- Students may find internships through a dedicated campus office
- Career centers typically manage internship advertising and tracking, act as liaisons between departments and host organizations, facilitate decisions on course credit, and offer scholarships for unpaid internships

How do you find host organizations?

- Approach the campus internship or career center to identify internship opportunities
- Reach out through your department's alumni network
- Take advantage of instructor contacts in organizations and communities
- Search online, including for specific organizations—local to global
- Rely on the initiative of individual students and their peer networks

- Do the legwork and build your own relationships with particular organizations

How do you vet and evaluate potential internship hosts?

- Make at least one site visit to begin developing relationships with members of the host organization, observe aspects of its organizational culture, gain insight into the host organization's interest in internships, and discuss the intern's potential contributions

    - A supervisor from the host organization will need to allocate time to support an intern (e.g., with training, mentoring)
    - Work tools for the intern will be necessary (e.g., computer, computer access)
    - **Ask:** To what extent does the host-organization supervisor understand that the learning component of the internship is at least as important as the intern's contributions to the host organization?

- When a site visit is not possible, frequent and early communication between the university and host organization may be an option

- Universities may have their own permission systems:

    - San Jose State University has two paths for approving host organizations depending on whether the internships are associated with course credit

What is involved in preparing for individual internships?

- To maximize student choices, it is best if internship planning occurs early in the program

    - Reminders to students from instructors and department advisors are helpful

- Time is necessary to search for appropriate placements, conduct informational interviews, and/or attend job/internship fairs on campus

    - Students can be directed to the campus career center for assistance

- Internship deadlines may have a long lead time: many organizations have their own fiscal and bureaucratic cycles that do not align well with academic terms

- To meet organizational deadlines, students will need to develop and submit resumes and cover letters

  - Campus career center professionals, along with instructor input are useful

- At the interview stage, applicants should practice their responses to interview questions and get feedback from peers and instructors

  - Mock interview sessions can improve student confidence

What are some helpful strategies when setting up an internship program?

Develop a **departmental template** on **internship planning** that consists of learning objectives and basic internship parameters. If necessary, the template can be customized for individual students. This short document will help guide conversations with students and host organizations. Consider these steps:

- **Gather student resumes and cover letters**

- **Articulate intern learning objectives**

  - Skill development and/or refinement
  - Acquisition of professionalization skills (e.g., decision making, problem solving, teamwork)
  - Timely completion of work tasks
  - Expansion of professional networks

- **Agree on the internship parameters**

  - Length of internship
  - Number of internship hours
  - Provision of work tools (e.g., laptop, special software)
  - Specific learning opportunities (per learning objectives)
  - Compensation from host organization, university course credit, or both

- Internship assessment: who will do it, how it will happen, and when it will happen
  - Roles and responsibilities of the university and host supervisors

- **Determine if the intern will engage in research and if so,**

  - Will Institutional Research Board approval be required?
  - Will the university or the host organization secure the necessary permissions?

How do we manage the diverse range of possible internships?

Develop a **departmental template** for a **written internship agreement** signed by all parties. It should be finalized before the internship is approved for credit (at or before the beginning of the term). An internship agreement does not need to be long (about one page) or complicated but should include:

- Contact information for the intern, host supervisor, and academic supervisor

- A brief, clear description of intern work duties drafted by the host supervisor with feedback from the intern and academic supervisor

- A short, clear academic statement of how this internship builds on or enhances experience relevant to anthropology (including learning outcomes) which can be drafted by the academic supervisor or the intern, with feedback from the other party

- A work schedule showing the total planned hours for the term

- Particularly for graduate students, a list of products (e.g., thesis, marketing plan, customer survey summary, board presentation) that are anticipated from the internship

How do we evaluate the student's work in the internship?

- The host supervisor prepares a brief written evaluation of the intern's work

- The intern composes a brief summary report with reflections on the experience, goals achieved, challenges faced, and ties to anthropology

- The intern maintains a log of internship hours

- These forms of evaluation are useful information for the intern, academic supervisor, and host organization. The most challenging part is getting all this information before the end of the term!

How do we raise the visibility of our internship program?

- Post on the department's website, as does the University of North Texas:

Undergraduate Research/Internship Opportunities | Department of Anthropology

> **ANTH 4920 Internship in Anthropology**
>
> The Department of Anthropology is happy to consider course credit for undergraduate internship experiences. Students who have been accepted into either a paid or unpaid internship program are encouraged to apply for academic credit. "Internship programs" may be defined in various ways, please consult with the department for questions regarding what constitutes an "internship".

- Recognize interns at your awards and recognition ceremonies, inviting host supervisors to attend

- Ask interns to write a short, bulleted summary of the value of their internship to be shared with future interns; consider posting these summaries on the department's website

- Highlight selected internship experiences with prospective students and their parents

35. Post-Internship Evaluation Guide

Sarah Heinemeier

Your internship program is off to a great start, but you want to evaluate your success. This guide shows you how to develop an actionable evaluation process for your internship program. As the job market and economy shift, it is important to keep current with emerging market expectations. Based on input from your interns, host organizations, and university/program, you should 1) assess the extent to which your program meets or exceeds the following criteria, and 2) apply that input to implement improvements in the program.

Internship Program Expectations	Apply Results to:
Interns • Gained valuable experiences and skills • Improved their ability to apply their skills in new contexts • Developed confidence in making and defending project-related decisions • Expanded their professional networks • Strengthened their understanding how they translate theory into practice • Enhanced their ability to identify opportunities for their own growth and professional development • Came to appreciate professional/trade associations and conferences, and/or news/publication outlets • Built confidence in speaking about or presenting their work • Learned to use their internships as stepping stones to new professional opportunities • Increased awareness of anthropology's workforce relevance and potential	Improve guidance and support for interns on anticipated experiences and new skill acquisition during the internship period Create follow-up skills or professional development for interns Enhance job placement support for interns
Host Organization • Improved the applicant pool for new hires • Identified tangible organizational benefits based on the work of interns • Strengthened their working relationship with the university/program • Leveraged the internship program into other university/program projects (e.g., invitation to deliver public lecture, award sponsorship) • Talked about hiring anthropologists in the future • Decided to continue working with interns	Establish clear workplace expectations for new interns Provide greater oversight and assistance throughout the internship period Alert intern's advisor of any work-related issues, as appropriate
University / Program • Gained prestige for implementing a high-leverage internship program • Strengthened their working relationships with the host organization • Leveraged the internship program into other activities with the host organization (e.g., invitation to deliver public lecture, award sponsorship) • Expanded the number of summer interns	Refine internship selection and placement processes Enhance university/program marketing and public relations

Crafting Your Internship Program Evaluation

Pick from the following question bank to create intern and host organization surveys and interviews. Select those questions that are most relevant for your program goals. The results from these surveys and interviews will help you determine whether you are meeting the criteria you established.

What we need to know	Options for Data Collection	Questions	Options for Question Format
To what extent did interns gain valuable skills?	Intern Survey or Interview	What skill or skills were you hoping to develop through this internship?	Open-ended "Choose all that apply"
	Intern Survey or Interview	Please describe all of the skills you were able to develop through the internship.	Open-ended
	Intern Survey or Interview	Did your internship help you develop these skills?	Five-point Likert scale of Strongly Agree to Strongly Disagree
	Intern Survey or Interview	For each skill, did your internship increase your proficiency in that skill?	Five-point Likert scale of Strongly Agree to Strongly Disagree
	Intern Survey or Interview	What were the best aspects of your internship experience?	Open-ended
	Intern Survey or Interview	What were the most challenging aspects of your internship experience?	Open-ended
	Host Organization Survey or Interview	What skills was the internship designed to help interns develop?	Open-ended "Choose all that apply"
	Host Organization Survey or Interview	Did your intern develop or improve the skills that the internship was designed to support?	Five-point Likert scale of Strongly Agree to Strongly Disagree • If Strongly Agree/Agree—What skills did you observe? • If Strongly Disagree/Disagree—Provide more feedback and suggestions for improvement
	Host Organization Survey or Interview	Were any additional skills developed?	Open-ended
	Host Organization Survey or Interview	For each skill, did the internship increase your intern's proficiency in that skill?	Five-point Likert scale of Strongly Agree to Strongly Disagree

What we need to know	Options for Data Collection	Questions	Options for Question Format
To what extent did interns improve their ability to apply their skills in new contexts?	Intern Survey or Interview	Were you given an opportunity to apply your skills on projects or in particular situations (e.g., interactions, meetings)?	Five-point Likert scale of Strongly Agree to Strongly Disagree • If Strongly Agree/Agree—Please describe • If Strongly Disagree/Disagree—Why not? What factors constrained your ability to apply your skills further?
	Intern Survey or Interview	Were you successful in applying your skills in those particular situations?	Five-point Likert scale of Strongly Agree to Strongly Disagree
	Host Organization Survey or Interview	Was your intern given an opportunity to apply their skills in particular situations (e.g., interactions, meetings)?	Five-point Likert scale of Strongly Agree to Strongly Disagree • If Strongly Agree/Agree—Please describe • If Strongly Disagree/Disagree—Why not? What factors constrained your ability to apply your skills further?
	Host Organization Survey or Interview	Was your intern successful in applying their skills in particular situations (e.g., interactions, meetings)?	Five-point Likert scale of Strongly Agree to Strongly Disagree
To what extent did interns develop confidence in making and defending project-related decisions?	Intern Survey or Interview	Were you given the opportunity to make decisions on your project?	Five-point Likert scale of Strongly Agree to Strongly Disagree • If Strongly Agree/Agree—Please describe how
	Intern Survey or Interview	Were you asked to defend or justify your decisions? If so, please describe this experience.	Y / N Open-ended
	Intern Survey or Interview	Comparing BEFORE (pre-internship) & NOW (post-internship): To what extent do you agree with the statement, "I am confident in making and defending project-related decisions"?	Five-point Likert scale of Strongly Agree to Strongly Disagree
	Host Organization Survey or Interview	Was your intern given the opportunity to make decisions on their project?	Five-point Likert scale of Strongly Agree to Strongly Disagree • If Strongly Agree/Agree—Please describe • If Strongly Disagree/Disagree—Why not?
	Host Organization Survey or Interview	Was your intern asked to defend or justify their project-related decisions? If so, please describe how the intern responded to this opportunity.	Y / N Open-ended

What we need to know	Options for Data Collection	Questions	Options for Question Format
To what extent did interns expand their professional networks?	Intern Survey or Interview	Comparing BEFORE (pre-internship) & NOW (post-internship): Did your professional contacts expand through: • Your LinkedIn profile • Number of working anthropologists • Social media presence (Facebook, Instagram, X) • Membership in one or more professional associations • Attendance at one or more annual conferences • Participation in a Community of Practice or Professional Learning Community • Relationship with a formal mentor or advisor • Book Club or Reading Circle • Other	Five-point Likert scale of Strongly Agree to Strongly Disagree
To what extent did interns strengthen their understanding of how they translate theory into practice?	Intern Survey or Interview	Has your understanding of how to translate theory into practice improved?	Five-point Likert scale of Strongly Agree to Strongly Disagree • If Strongly Agree/Agree—Please describe • If Strongly Disagree/Disagree—Why not?
	Host Organization Survey or Interview	Has your intern's understanding of how to translate theory into practice improved?	Five-point Likert scale of Strongly Agree to Strongly Disagree • If Strongly Agree/Agree—Please describe • If Strongly Disagree/Disagree—Why not?
To what extent did interns enhance their ability to identify growth or professional development opportunities	Intern Survey or Interview	Describe a task or activity that did not go as you thought it would or as you planned. What did you learn as a result?	Open-ended
	Host Organization Survey or Interview	Describe a task or activity (in which your intern had meaningful involvement or responsibility) that did not go as you thought it would or as you planned. What did your intern learn as a result?	Open-ended

What we need to know	Options for Data Collection	Questions	Options for Question Format
To what extent did interns learn how to access and use associations, conferences, and news/publication outlets?	Intern Survey or Interview	Comparing BEFORE (pre-internship) & NOW (post-internship): Did you learn how to access and use: • Professional associations • Trade associations • Professional conferences • Trade conferences • Academic publications • News outlets • Other (Please specify)	Five-point Likert scale of Strongly Agree to Strongly Disagree
To what extent did interns build confidence in speaking about or presenting their work?	Intern Survey or Interview	Has your confidence improved in speaking about or presenting your work?	Five-point Likert scale of Strongly Agree to Strongly Disagree • If Strongly Agree/Agree—Please describe • If Strongly Disagree/Disagree—Why not?
	Intern Survey or Interview	Comparing BEFORE (pre-internship) & NOW (post-internship): To what extent do you agree with the statement, "I am confident in speaking about or presenting my work"?	Five-point Likert scale of Strongly Agree to Strongly Disagree
	Host Organization Survey or Interview	Has your intern's confidence in speaking about or presenting their work improved?	Five-point Likert scale of Strongly Agree to Strongly Disagree • If Strongly Agree/Agree—Please describe • If Strongly Disagree/Disagree—Why not?
To what extent have interns been able to use their internship as a stepping stone to new professional opportunities?	Intern Survey or Interview	Have you been able to translate your internship into an ongoing or longer-term opportunity?	❏ Yes ❏ No ❏ In Progress ❏ Unsure • If Yes or In Progress, please provide more details about your opportunity.

What we need to know	Options for Data Collection	Questions	Options for Question Format
To what extent have interns improved their awareness of anthropology's workforce relevance or potential?	Intern Survey or Interview	To what extent has your awareness about anthropology as an important or useful career changed?	❑ My awareness has improved and my opinion about anthropology as a career is now more positive ❑ My awareness has improved but my opinion about anthropology as a career has not changed ❑ My awareness has improved but my opinion about anthropology as a career is now more negative ❑ My awareness about anthropology as a career has not changed based on this internship ❑ Unsure ❑ Not Applicable • If "My awareness has improved but my opinion about anthropology as a career has not changed" OR "My awareness has improved but my opinion about anthropology as a career is now more negative," please provide more details about your experience.
To what extent did host organizations improve their applicant pool for new hires?	Host Organization Survey or Interview	To what extent do you agree the internship program helped improve the pool of applicants at your organization?	Five-point Likert scale of Strongly Agree to Strongly Disagree • If Strongly Agree/Agree—Please describe • If Strongly Disagree/Disagree—Why not? ❑ Unsure—I am not connected with hiring
To what extent did host organizations identify tangible organizational benefits based on the work of interns?	Host Organization Survey or Interview	To what extent do you agree the internship program brought new perspectives or skills to your team?	Five-point Likert scale of Strongly Agree to Strongly Disagree • If Strongly Agree/Agree—Please describe

What we need to know	Options for Data Collection	Questions	Options for Question Format
To what extent did host organizations talk about hiring anthropologists in the future?	Host Organization Survey or Interview	To what extent do you agree that the internship program has cultivated conversations about hiring anthropologists in the future?	Five-point Likert scale of Strongly Agree to Strongly Disagree • If Strongly Agree/Agree—Please describe • If Strongly Disagree/Disagree—Why not?
To what extent did host organizations strengthen their working relationships with the university or program?	Host Organization Survey or Interview	To what extent do you agree the internship program has strengthened your working relationship with the university or program?	Five-point Likert scale of Strongly Agree to Strongly Disagree • If Strongly Agree/Agree—Please describe • If Strongly Disagree/Disagree—Why not?
To what extent did host organizations leverage the internship program into other university/program projects (e.g., sponsorship of lecture series, other funded initiative)?	Host Organization Survey or Interview	Has the internship program led to other collaborations with the university or program? If so, what is the nature of those collaborations?	Open-ended Close-ended if we can identify specific projects of interest

What we need to know	Options for Data Collection	Questions	Options for Question Format
To what extent will host organizations continue working with interns?	Host Organization Survey or Interview	Would you participate in an internship program again?	❏ Yes ❏ Definitely not ❏ Maybe, if certain changes were made ❏ Unsure at present ❏ Not Applicable • If "Definitely Not," please provide more details about your experience. • If "Maybe, if certain changes were made," please indicate the changes that are needed. • If "Unsure at present," please indicate the factors that might affect your decision.
	Host Organization Survey or Interview	How can the department/internship director support your organization in the future?	Open-ended Close-ended (if we can identify specific projects of interest)
	Host Organization Survey or Interview	How might the department ensure a better fit between your organization and any interns?	Open-ended Close-ended (if we can identify specific projects of interest)
	Host Organization Survey or Interview	Is there any capability you wish your intern had had (e.g., classwork, experience) before starting the internship?	Open-ended Close-ended (if we can identify specific projects of interest)
To what extent did the university or program gain prestige for implementing a high-leverage internship program?	University Survey or Interview	Has the internship program led to greater prestige for your university or program?	Five-point Likert scale of Strongly Agree to Strongly Disagree • If Strongly Agree/Agree—Please describe • If Strongly Disagree/Disagree—Why not?

What we need to know	Options for Data Collection	Questions	Options for Question Format
To what extent did the university or program strengthen their working relationship with the host organization?	University Survey or Interview	Has the internship program strengthened your relationship with your host organization?	Five-point Likert scale of Strongly Agree to Strongly Disagree • If Strongly Agree/Agree—Please describe • If Strongly Disagree/Disagree—Why not?
To what extent did the university or program leverage the internship program into other activities with the host organization?	University Survey or Interview	Has the internship program led to other collaborations with the host organization? If so, what is the nature of those collaborations?	Open-ended Close-ended (if we can identify specific projects of interest)
To what extent did the university or program expand the number of interns?	University Survey or Interview	Has the annual number of interns increased?	Open-ended

Analyze and Act!

Once you have collected your surveys and interviews, analyze the results and discover where you can take action. Prioritize your results based on their urgency and importance. There may be changes you can implement right away, while others may take additional planning or resources. Credit the feedback you received from your interns, hosts, and university when sharing and communicating your changes. Your response to these key stakeholders demonstrates that you are listening and acting based on their input. If people can see their impact, you have a better chance of them responding to a future survey or interview request.

36. Making Career Fairs Work for Anthropologists

Robert McCallum

College career fairs are excellent occasions for students to meet and network with potential employers and lay the groundwork for possible employment opportunities. Often held twice during the academic year, these career fairs, also present opportunities for students to conduct fieldwork, investigating at these events and incorporating what they learn into their own internship or job search. This tool outlines both research and practice activities that can be integrated within selected courses (e.g., methods, applied anthropology, professionalization) or explored by individual students on their own. The following activities are designed to help students prepare for and get the most out of career fairs.

Be an Anthropologist: Conduct a Mini Ethnography

A career fair provides real-world anthropology experience while helping students prepare for their own job search. Frame career fairs as unfamiliar environments with their own purposes, cultural norms, signs and symbols, and language. Have students develop and execute a research plan using their ethnographic skills (e.g., observation, intercept interviews in which they approach people to ask a few questions). Students can use the questions below to get started.

What happens at a career fair?

- *Observation*: How do student attendees interact with recruiters? Who leads the conversation? To what extent do the attendees talk about themselves? Are any "artifacts" (e.g., resumes, business cards) part of interactions with recruiters? What seems to pique recruiter interest? What information can be derived from nonverbal signals (e.g., clothing, accessories, physical appearance, stance)?

- **_Participant observation_**: Recruiters are gatekeepers. When they are not busy, have students chat with them to practice developing rapport. Students can ask questions about the recruiters' job and probe about their goals, what they value in career fairs and their own career, and how they define success. These conversations represent a chance to learn about unspoken rules and expectations within organizations.

- **_Intercept interviews_ _with recruiters_**: Why does their organization have a career-fair presence? What are all the goals they hope to achieve? Do they have any openings for internships, or part-time or full-time employment? How long have they been engaged in career fairs? Is there anything special about this particular career fair?

- **_Intercept interviews with student attendees_**: Why are they attending this event? What did they do to prepare for this event? Have they attended career fairs before? What are the best questions to ask recruiters? What are the "rules" for interacting effectively with recruiters?

What does an organization expect to gain by participating in a career fair?

- **_Walk-around survey_** (_as the event is getting set up or beginning_): What organizations have booths at the career fair? How many booths are there? What "artifacts" are included as part of each booth?

- **_Interviews with recruiters_** (_prior to the event_): What are all the reasons an organization has a booth at the career fair? How much preparation is required to have a successful event? What elements contribute to a successful career fair? What questions does the recruiter typically ask the student attendees? What attributes does the recruiter hope to see in these students? How does the recruiter rank attendees? What pushes these attendees along the journey to an internship or full-time employment? Are there attributes or behaviors that reduce the likelihood of being hired? Are there benefits of a career fair interaction over a virtual interview with a job candidate?

- **_Interviews with university staff_** (_prior to the event_): What are all the reasons the university hosts career fairs? How much university time is required to have a successful event? What elements contribute to a successful career fair? Does the university conduct evaluations of their career fairs? What is that evaluation process like? To what extent does the university use evaluation input to design subsequent career fairs?

How does a college in-person career fair compare with other job recruitment events (e.g., online career fairs, one-on-one recruiter interviews)?

- *Observation*: What are some similarities? What are some differences?

- *Participant observation*: What questions arose during any discussions? What insights can be gleaned from these experiences? How can participation enhance or shift one's understanding of recruiting and hiring practices?

Get Involved in the Job Market

Encourage students to actively seek a summer internship or full-time job after graduation at a career fair. This activity offers practice in establishing rapport with recruiters, preparing and delivering their resume, preparing and performing their elevator pitch, interacting effectively with recruiters, and closing the discussion with a plan to follow up. Students can:

Develop application materials

- Review the tool <u>Distinguishing Resumes, CVs, Portfolios, and Bios</u>

- Have students get a professional-looking headshot photo, see the tool <u>Creating an Effective Professional Headshot</u>

- Seek support from your campus Career Services for developing application materials

- In class, strategize ways to help recruiters remember them and their resumes (e.g., business cards with a memorable phrase)

Prepare an elevator pitch

- Review the tool <u>Mastering the Elevator Pitch</u>

- Have students practice elevator pitches first with peers and then with professionals

- Ensure they reflect upon and gather all input to improve content and delivery

- Look for workshops offered by Career Services to help practice and develop how students introduce themselves to potential employers

Participate in mock interviews

- Review the tool on <u>Professional Etiquette for In-Person and Remote Meetings</u>

- Use AI to ask interview questions based on questions likely to be asked at a career fair; create an additional prompt for "curveball" questions that might be less common but plausible

  Note: Universities often offer platforms such as <u>Big Interview</u> with interview practice tools that are free

- Hold mock interviews in class in which the students take turns role playing either the recruiter or the student; discuss what each party learned

- Bring in an experienced professional (e.g., professional recruiter, campus Career Services staff) to class to conduct mock interviews with the students and provide feedback

Do self-evaluation

- Ask students to reflect on how they think they will come across to potential employers; have them think about first impressions, how they will talk about themselves: their skills, knowledge, and experiences

- Have students find someone they trust to talk with and provide feedback

Attend a career fair and engage with recruiters

- Assign students to find a list of employers attending the fair (which are often published before the event). Research the ones of interest prior to the career fair by visiting their websites and social media, reviewing their mission and values, and learning about current job openings

- Discuss how best to dress since this will be the first impression, before they even say a word, to a recruiter; students should choose business-professional or business-casual attire as if they were going to an interview, avoiding more casual wear like ripped jeans, gym shorts, rubber flip-flops, and going easy on cologne or perfume

Note: When students look professional, they will feel more confident, and recruiters will be more likely to take them seriously as job/internship candidates.

- Suggest students approach recruiters from a couple of organizations where they have the least amount of interest to get comfortable and "warm up" and then move on to organizations they are interested in; students should always remain open minded to potential opportunities at any organization

- Challenge students to have meaningful conversations, inquiring about open roles, internships, ideal candidate attributes, and the organizational culture

- Encourage students to stay aware of their surroundings (e.g., when there is a line, keep the conversation targeted and brief; if the booth is quiet, take the opportunity to ask more in-depth questions and build rapport) and engage with others instead of looking at their phones

- Require four to five of these interactions with recruiters, encouraging them to ask about the best way to follow-up with the organization

- After each interaction, ensure students reflect on what went well and what needs improvement

    Tip: Students should jot down important notes about the organizations and recruiters since referencing names and what they know about the organization could be helpful in later parts of the application process

- End with participant observation. Take advantage of the opportunity to hang out and continue to observe and ask questions of any attendees and recruiters at the career fair

Debrief

- Hold a meet up immediately after the career fair to talk about their experiences

- Set aside time in class to capture these lessons

- Assign students to write an essay about how their approach to their next recruiter interview or career fair will change based on what they learned

Reach out to recruiters/talent acquisition specialists at organizations on LinkedIn in which they are interested

- Suggest students request an <u>informational interview</u> with these recruiters to talk about what they look for in candidates

- Incorporate what they learned into their next job search activities

- Connect with fellow alumni who work at the organizations they are interested in for informational interviews. They can use LinkedIn, <u>PeopleGrove</u>, or any available alumni connection portals

37. Creating an Implementation Plan for Action

Riall W. Nolan

Ideas are great, but at some point, they need to be implemented. And for that, you need a plan.

You may have used other ACRN tools to help you identify some broad goals for your department (e.g., Putting Force Field Analysis to Work). You now need to turn those high-level goals into clear objectives—specific and measurable actions—and draw up an implementation plan for achieving them.

Objectives are smaller than goals, more concrete and more limited in scope. A broad goal may have half a dozen objectives embedded within it. Since a particular goal can probably be reached in several different ways, developing objectives which align to target the overall goal work best. Each can be described in a one-sentence objective statement.

Characteristics of Strong Objective Statements

Draft clear objective statements that resonate with you and your colleagues. Objective statements usually begin with the word "To," followed by an action verb. Objective statements are positive and declarative. They illustrate a future state and describe "what," "when," and "how much?" Strong objective statements are SMART:

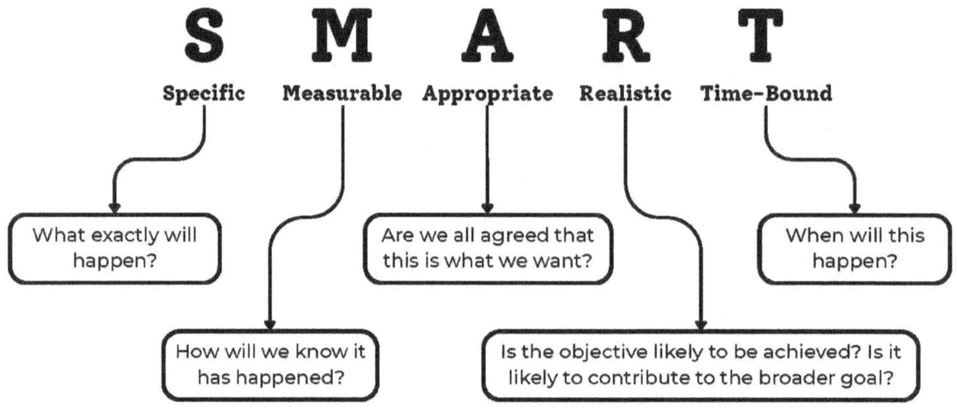

For example, if a person's goal was to conduct more collaborative research, one of their objectives might be, "To submit two conference session proposals with colleagues in the next academic year."

Different Types of Objectives

Several types of objectives[1] have been identified:

TYPE	HOW MEASURED	EXAMPLE
QUANTITATIVE	Deterministically: with specific numerical values Probabilistically: with approximate numerical values	"To achieve a score of 75% on today's math test." "To achieve a score of 70% or higher on today's math test."
QUALITATIVE	Subjectively: according to axiomatic principles	"To be chosen as Most Valuable Player this year."
BINARY-EVENT	Logically: according to observed events	"To land the aircraft on the carrier's flight deck in the next ten minutes."

Your Implementation Plan

An implementation plan helps you achieve your objectives. It is simple and provides information about several aspects of your objectives:

- Activities to be carried out
- Resources needed for these activities
- Responsibilities of the various actors
- Timetable to be followed
- Indicators you will use to measure success
- Means of verification you will use (i.e., where will you get the indicators)
- Key assumptions which may affect outcomes.

Here is some additional detail on these elements:

Activities: Activities are actions that are taken to reach an objective. If any seem difficult or complicated, try working backwards from the final 'deliverable,' listing each step in reverse order.

Keep your description at a relatively crude level of detail—accurate enough to distinguish between major categories of effort, but not so detailed that you lose yourself in minutiae.

Resources: All activities require resources including time, money, personnel, equipment, and information. You should (a) list the needed resources; (b) provide as much detail as you can; (c) determine whether you already have what you need; or (d) specify what else you need. If money is involved, then you will also need some sort of budget.

Actors: Who will engage in these activities? An implementation plan enables your department to discuss, modify, and reach consensus about what needs doing by whom. Usually, more than one person is involved. If the tasks are complex or unfamiliar, make sure that everyone knows what to do. For brand-new ventures, some training may be necessary.

Timetables: For simple sets of activities, it is probably enough to mark the main events on your calendar. For other activities, it is useful to have a more detailed method of scheduling. Gantt charts are one model. They will suffice for relatively straightforward tasks. PERT charts are a different model. They can help you understand the linkages between sets of activities and where crunch points are likely to surface.

Indicators: How will you know you have succeeded? Your indicators will tell you. They should be tangible and represent convincing evidence of success. They should be specific to the effort at hand. Most importantly, they should be plausible, in that they will be accepted as valid by different people.

Means of Verification: How will you get your indicators? Will you need to collect data? Will you access data available elsewhere? For example, if one of your key indicators is increased student majors, how will you know? What evidence will you cite? All your indicators should be both obtainable without undue extra effort, and plausible, in the sense that they are objectively verifiable and accepted as valid.

Key Assumptions: These are factors necessary for success but essentially outside your planning framework. Only some of them can be controlled by your department. Regardless of your ability to control these factors, you need to be aware of them, and monitor them if necessary.

An Implementation Plan Example

Each participating anthropology department/program in ACRN's <u>Departmental Advisory Initiative (DAI)</u> submits a career readiness implementation plan once the site visit to the university has concluded. The Department presents its plan and receives feedback from ACRN leaders. Once the plan is finalized, the work of implementing the plan begins.

Here is an example of a DAI implementation plan. The table identifies six objectives related to the goal of strengthening career readiness. Typically, Key Assumptions have their own column in an implementation plan since they may affect any or all outcomes. However, in this case, department members exert most of the control over these objectives. Consequently, we did not include Key Assumptions in the table.

Reference
1. Delp, P., A. Thesen, J. Motiwalla, and N. Seshadri. 1977. Delphi System Tools for Project Planning, Columbus, OH: National Center for Research in Vocational Education, Ohio State University, 45-56.

Objective	Activities	Resources	Actors	Timetable	Indicators	Means of Verification
Begin planning ANTH Advisory Committee	**1.** Develop specs **2.** Identify 4-5 people **3.** Contact them **4.** Schedule meeting for Fall 2025	LinkedIn	Dept. Chair	**1.** End Fall 2024 **2.** Early Spring 2025 **3.** End Spring 2025 **4.** End Spring 2025	4-5 people agree to serve	First ANTH Advisory Committee meeting takes place with 4-5 members
Enhance skill building in all BA courses	**1.** Look at ACRN Job Seeker and Career Tools, **2.** Instructor Tools, and Speakers Bureau **3.** Identify current skill-building assignment **4.** Each instructor figures out how to present Work toward a panel for majors	• ACRN tool: Identify and Rate Your Skills • Pre and post questions • sNAPAshots • LinkedIn	Each instructor	**1.** First week of Spring 2025 to discuss within Dept. **2.** First week of Spring 2025 to discuss within Dept. **3.** Roll out in course Assess/revise for Fall 25	• Each instructor pilots in one course Spring 25 • Do in all Fall 2025 courses	• Each instructor verifies that skill building has been integrated into all courses • Students surveyed indicate skill building was part of each course
Build connection with local organizations	**1.** Explore Handshake **2.** Contact 2-3 alums who work or interned in these local organizations	• Alumni • Businesses • Nonprofits • Government • Global Philanthropy Alliance	Two instructors	**1.** Early Spring 2025 **2.** Make contact in early Spring 2025	Connect with at least two organizations by end of fall 2025	• Instructors report on interactions
Student-alumni interviews in Ethnographic Film Course	**1.** Students interview 3-4 alumni across subfields **2.** Post videos to Dept. webpages	Video equipment already secured	Instructor teaching Ethnographic Film Course	**1.** Film Spring 2025 **2.** Post by Fall 2025	• 3-4 interviews conducted • 3-4 videos created	• 3-4 interviews completed • 3-4 videos created and posted to ANTH webpages
Enhance Professionalization course	**1.** Students create their LinkedIn profiles **2.** Students conduct an informational interview **3.** Get copy of Career Tools for Anthropology book	ACRN website	Instructor teaching Professionalization course	**1.** Spring 2025 **2.** Spring 2025 **3.** Spring 2025	• Student profiles are finished • Informational interview is completed	• Student profiles on LinkedIn Group are verified • Video recording of informational interview is available for viewing
Create one-credit IRB course	Outline of the course is drafted, and proposal written	Instructor serves on IRB Committee	Instructor is serving on IRB Committee	Summer 2025	Curriculum and Academic Policies Council (CAPC) proposal is completed	Proposal is submitted to CAPC

REFERENCES

Artz, Matt and Lora Koycheva, eds. 2025. *EmTech Anthropology: Careers at the Frontier*. New York, NY: Taylor & Francis.

Briody, Elizabeth K. 1995. "Making *Anthropologists at Work*: Lessons for Anthropologists," *Practicing Anthropology*, 17(1&2), Winter/Spring: 32-36.

Davis, Nancy Yaw, Roger P. McConochie, and David R. Stevenson. 1987. *Research and Consulting as a Business*. NAPA Bulletin 4, American Anthropological Association.

Fiske, Shirley J., Linda A. Bennett, Patricia Ensworth, Terry Redding, and Keri Brondo. 2010. "The Changing Face of Anthropology: Anthropology Masters Reflect on Education, Careers, and Professional Organizations." *AAA/CoPAPIA 2009 Anthropology MA Career Survey*. Arlington, VA: American Anthropological Association.

Guerrón Montero, Carla, ed. 2008. *Careers in Applied Anthropology in the 21st Century; Perspectives from Academics and Practitioners*. NAPA Bulletin 29. American Anthropological Association.

Hanson, Karen J., John J. Conway, Jack Alexander, and H. Max Drake. 1988. *Mainstreaming Anthropology: Experiences in Government Employment*. NAPA Bulletin 5, American Anthropological Association.

Hawvermale, Erica, Shannon Cronin, Kayla Davis, Janice Byth, Brynn Torres, Gi Giamargo, Leyla Koyuncuoglu, Sarah Stutts, and Ky Burke. 2020. "The Face of Anthropology One Decade Later: Anthropology Master's Reflections on Education, Careers, and Professional Organizations Then and Now," *2019 American Anthropology Master's Career Survey*. Arlington, VA: American Anthropological Association.

Irwin, V., Wang, K., Tezil, T., Zhang, J., Filbey, A., Jung, J., Bullock Mann, F., Dilig, R., and Parker, S. 2023. *Report on the Condition of Education 2023 (NCES 2023-144)*. U.S. Department of Education. Washington, DC: National Center for Education Statistics. Retrieved [date] from https://nces.ed.gov/pubsearch/pubsinfo.asp?pubid=2023144.

Meerwarth, Tracy L., Julia C. Gluesing, and Brigitte Jordan. 2008. *Mobile Work, Mobile Lives: Cultural Accounts of Lived Experiences*. NAPA Bulletin 30, American Anthropological Association.

Nolan, Riall W., ed. 2013. *A Handbook of Practicing Anthropology*. Malden, MA: Wiley-Blackwell.

Nolan, Riall W. 2026. *Using Anthropology in the World: A Guide to Becoming an Anthropologist Practitioner*. 2nd ed. New York, NY: Taylor & Francis.

Nolan, Riall W. and Elizabeth K. Briody. 2023. "A Career Ready Curriculum for Anthropologists," *Practicing Anthropology*, 45(3): 26-30, Summer, 2023. DOI: 10.17730/0888-4552.45.3.26.

Nolan, Riall W. and Elizabeth K. Briody. 2024. "How Career Ready Are Your Students? Reflections on What We Are (Not) Teaching Anthropology Students," *Annals of Anthropological Practice*, 48(1): 5-19, May 2024, DOI: 10.1111/napa.12209.

Oliveira, Pedro. 2013. *People-Centered Innovation: Becoming a Practitioner in Innovation Research*. Columbus, OH: Biblio Publishing.

Podjed, Dan and Carla Guerrón Montero. 2026. *Why the World Needs Anthropologists*. 2nd ed. New York, NY: Taylor & Francis.

Ramer, Angela, Jenell Paris, Peter Van Arsdale, Sergio Lopez, Stephen L. Schensul, and David Flood. 2022. Departmental Experience with Application and Practice. https://anthrocareerready.net/wp-content/uploads/2022/07/Gr-4-Dept.-Exp.-w-Practice-072622.pdf

Reed, Michael C., ed. 1997. *Practicing Anthropology in a Postmodern World: Lessons and Insights from Federal Contract Research*. NAPA Bulletin 17. American Anthropological Association.

Sabloff, Paula L.W., ed. 2000. *Careers in Anthropology: Profiles of Practitioner Anthropologists*. NAPA Bulletin 20. American Anthropological Association.

Strang, Veronica. 2021. *What Anthropologists Do*. 2nd ed. London, UK: Taylor & Francis.

Trester, Anna Marie. 2022. *Employing Linguistics: Thinking and Talking about Careers for Linguists*. London, UK: Bloomsbury Academic.

Wasson, Christina, ed. 2006. *Making History at the Frontier: Women Creating Careers as Practicing Anthropologists*. NAPA Bulletin 26. American Anthropological Association.

FURTHER RESOURCES

Other readings and resources are available for groups and individuals interested in promoting career readiness in their academic offerings.

BOOKS

Bakker, Laurens, Masja Cohen, and Walter Faaij. 2020. *Anthropologists Wanted: Why Organizations Need Anthropology.* Amsterdam, The Netherlands: Amsterdam University Press.

Briller, Sherrylyn H. and Amy Goldmacher. 2021. *Designing an Anthropology Career: Professional Development Exercises.* 2nd ed. Lanham, MD: Rowman & Littlefield.

Camenson, Blythe. 2005. *Great Jobs for Anthropology Majors.* McGraw Hill Professional.

Ellick, Carol J. and Joe E. Watkins. 2011. *The Anthropology Graduate's Guide: From Student to a Career.* New York, NY: Taylor & Francis.

Koycheva, Lora, Angela K. VandenBroek, and Matt Artz, eds. 2026. *Anthropology and AI.* London, UK: Routledge.

Nolan, Riall W. 2003. *Anthropology in Practice: Building a Career Outside the Academy.* Boulder, CO: Lynne Reinner Publishers.

Redding, Terry M. and Charles C. Cheney. 2022. *Profiles of Anthropological Praxis: An International Casebook.* New York, NY: Berghahn.

Studebaker, Jennifer, Elizabeth K. Briody, Zahra Malik, and Riall W. Nolan. 2024. *Career Tools for Anthropology: An Anthropology Career Readiness Network Workbook.* ACRN Press.

Wulff, Robert M. and Shirley J. Fiske, eds. 1987. *Anthropological Praxis: Translating Knowledge into Action.* Boulder, CO: Westview Press.

Wasson, Christina, ed. 2026. *Routledge Handbook of Applied Anthropology.* London, UK: Routledge.

VIDEOS

Altimare, Emily L. 2008. *Beyond Ethnography: Corporate and Design Anthropology*. Careers in Anthropology No. 2. American Anthropological Association. (https://youtu.be/sW5nP3ao--w)

Briody, Elizabeth K. and Dawn Bodo. 1994. *Anthropologists at Work: Careers Making a Difference.* American Anthropological Association and EXPOSE: Communications Network. (https://youtu.be/9S7QnAKZnOY)

Gamwell, Adam, Phil Surles, Elizabeth K. Briody, Dawn Lehman, and Jo Aiken. 2022. *Anthropologists on the Public Stage.* https://www.anthrocurious.com/courses

Smiley, Francis E. 2005. *Applying Anthropology: Careers That Count.* (https://youtu.be/HxyFwgV9PYQ)

sNAPAshots (2022-present). https://practicinganthropology.org/blog/snapashots-conversations-with-professional-practicing-and-applied-anthropologists/

PODCASTS

AnthroBiology Podcast: https://anthrobiology.com

AnthroPod: https://culanth.org/fieldsights/series/anthropod

Anthropuzzled Podcast: https://www.anthropuzzled.com

A Day in the Life of a Digital Anthropologist:

https://rss.com/podcasts/digitalanthropologist/

Linguistics Careercast: https://www.linguisticscareercast.com

Matt Artz Podcasts: https://www.mattartz.me/podcasts/

This Anthro Life: https://www.thisanthrolife.org

Anthropology in Practice Blog: https://anthropologyinpractice.com

The Conversation – Anthropology Section:

https://theconversation.com/us/topics/anthropology-92

World of Work Blog: https://anthrocareerready.net/updates/world-of-work-blog/

ASSOCIATIONS AND NETWORKS

American Anthropological Association (AAA): https://americananthro.org

Anthropology Career Readiness Network (ACRN): https://anthrocareerready.net

Anthropology in Praxis/Anthropologie Pratique (AP): https://anthropologyinpraxis.ca

Applied Anthropology Network (AAN): https://applied-anthropology.com

EPIC: https://www.epicpeople.org

High Plains Society for Applied Anthropology (HPSFAA): https://hpsfaa.wildapricot.org

Linguistics Career Launch:

https://docs.google.com/document/d/1JAGkt-CbFFH9aTFzqnbEqsGLEd79l1UsU2ev_J5tvrQ/edit?tab=t.0#heading=h.6jynaot9cbnq

National Association for the Practice of Anthropology (NAPA):

https://www.practicinganthropology.org

Society for Applied Anthropology (SfAA): https://www.appliedanthro.org

Washington Association of Professional Anthropologists (WAPA): https://wapadc.org

EDITORS' BIOS

Riall W. Nolan is Professor Emeritus of Anthropology at Purdue University. His current focus is on transforming anthropology into a force for good change, through the reform and revision of how we teach our students. He is Co-Chair of the Anthropology Career Readiness Network.

Irene Greene is an ACRN intern and a recent BA graduate from California State University, Northridge. Her interests lie in applied anthropology, organizational governance, and research. She will be pursuing a master's degree in Anthropology at The University of St Andrews.

Tereza Emilova is a UX researcher working in billing and payment management for digital products. She holds a Master's degree in Visual Anthropology from NOVA University Lisbon and has been supporting ACRN as an intern. Her interests include service design and the application of anthropological perspectives to complex systems.

Jennifer Studebaker is a business anthropologist based in Kansas City. She is the Executive Director of the Women, Food and Agriculture Network as well as the Founder of Studebaker Consulting LLC. Studebaker is a Co-Chair of the Anthropology Career Readiness Network.

Elizabeth K. Briody is Founder and Principal of Culture Keys LLC which assists organizations with cultural and change issues. She has been passionate about improving student career readiness for the workplace and is Co-Chair of the Anthropology Career Readiness Network.

AUTHORS' BIOS

Elizabeth K. Briody is Founder and Principal of Culture Keys LLC which assists organizations with cultural and change issues. Throughout her career, she has been passionate about improving student career readiness for the workplace and is Co-Chair of the Anthropology Career Readiness Network.

Keri Vacanti Brondo is the Lambros Comitas Chair of Applied Anthropology and Professor at Teachers College (TC), Columbia University. She has decades of leadership experience within anthropology's largest professional associations and has served in multiple administrative roles at the University of Memphis, including Chairperson and Associate Dean.

Barry Dornfeld is a principal and strategic advisor at the Center for Applied Research (CFAR), a consultancy specializing in organizational culture, change, strategy, leadership, and governance. He leads CFAR's Higher Education practice and advises leaders through complex strategic and organizational change, drawing on his training as an anthropologist in his consulting, teaching, and writing.

Ken C. Erickson recently retired as Associate Professor of International Business at the University of South Carolina. He operated an international ethnographic research firm for global clients for 15 years and is now Adjunct Professor of Anthropology at Eastern New Mexico University.

Jonathan Geyer is an MA candidate in Asian Studies at the Elliott School of International Affairs. He is also Assistant Director of ASEAN Affairs at the Organization of Asian Studies.

Irene Greene is an ACRN intern and a recent BA graduate from California State University, Northridge. Her interests lie in applied anthropology, organizational governance, and research. She will be pursuing a master's degree in Anthropology at The University of St Andrews.

Carla Guerrón Montero is an applied cultural anthropologist who studies how the constructed nature of heritage manifests in tourism, travel, and food within the African diaspora, as well as world anthropologies—anthropological theories created and practiced around the world. She is Professor of Anthropology and Director of the Center for Material Culture at the University of Delaware.

Sarah Heinemeier is a founding partner at Compass Evaluation and Research in Durham NC. She received her doctorate in Social Foundations of Education from the University of North Carolina at Chapel Hill. Since then, she has worked to assess early childhood and other educational initiatives and provides training and technical assistance on evaluation to non-profit, private, and educational agencies.

Aimee Huard has been awarded the CCSNH Chancellor's Award for Teaching Excellence and is currently Chair of the Social Science Department at Great BAY Community College in New Hampshire. Her research currently centers on utilizing anthropological methodologies to explore the connections of higher education and careers, ethical research, and the impact of GenAI on teaching and learning.

Ed Liebow served as Executive Director of the American Anthropological Association from 2012-2023, before which he conducted applied research for 27 years on a variety of environmental, public health, and social policy issues for the Battelle Memorial Institute.

Priscilla Rachun Linn, a museum anthropologist, developed and curated major exhibitions for the Smithsonian Institution, Hillwood Museum, and the League of Women Voters and help found the National Museum of American Diplomacy. In her retirement, she edits the World of Work Blog for ACRN.

Ted (Edward) Maclin is an anthropologist based at the University of Memphis. His work focuses on environmental justice, climate change, and the politics of technology. He has developed and led internship programs for youth and adults for over 30 years.

Zahra Malik, a People & Payroll Coordinator @ Displayco Canada, holds a BSc in Biological Anthropology and a Master of Management. Her interests lie in human behavior and social dynamics and how they inform organizational culture, strategy, and the application of anthropology in contemporary workplaces.

Jeff Martin is the Senior Director of External Relations for the American Anthropological Association. In addition to promoting the field to policy makers and the general public, he works with national and international publications including *CNN*, *NPR*, *The Wall St. Journal*, *The New York Times*, and *The Washington Post*.

Robert McCallum is a UX researcher and ethnographer at Meijer. He also conducted human-centered design research at Ford Motor Company and UX research in the tech space. Robert holds an MA in business and organizational anthropology from Wayne State University.

Janelle Moreno holds an MA in sociocultural anthropology and is based in Portland, OR. She works in supported employment, helping people with disabilities find and succeed in jobs, and promoting inclusive hiring.

Riall W. Nolan is Professor Emeritus of Anthropology at Purdue University. His current focus is on transforming anthropology into a force for good change, through the reform and revision of how we teach our students. He is Co-Chair of the Anthropology Career Readiness Network.

Megan O'Brien-Rene is an ACRN intern and graduate from California State University, Northridge, with research experience in policy, community-based participatory research, and cultural heritage. Using student focus groups, she gathered insights that were compiled into an ACRN tool aimed at increasing anthropology's visibility on campuses.

Emma Pramuk holds BA degrees in anthropology and journalism from the University of North Texas, where she explored how people, stories, and media intersect. She is passionate about community development and higher education and served as ACRN's Digital Marketing Intern.

Laurie Schwede, anthropologist, worked in the Census Bureau's research directorate, designing and testing questionnaires and leading short-term ethnographic evaluations during decennial censuses. She is a member of the Washington Association of Professional Anthropologists board and its Praxis Award Committee.

Susan Squires is associate professor in the Department of Anthropology at the University of North Texas. While she is best known for her expertise on customer insights research, she is currently using social network analysis for a study of Newfoundland fishing outports.

Kedron Thomas is an associate professor of anthropology at the University of Delaware. She is the author of *Regulating Style: Intellectual Property Law and the Business of Fashion in Guatemala.*

Jennifer Trivedi is an Associate Professor in Anthropology and a Core Faculty Member at the Disaster Research Center at the University of Delaware where she studies historical and cultural contexts surrounding disasters, including decision-making, timing, response, and recovery.

Andrew Walsh teaches in the Department of Anthropology at Western University in London, Ontario, Canada. His research, undertaken in collaboration with Malagasy NGOs and community associations, focuses largely on the impacts of global humanitarian and conservation interventions on communities in northern Madagascar.

Michael Wesch is Professor of Cultural Anthropology at Kansas State University and former US Professor of the Year, known for innovative teaching, ethnographic filmmaking, and author of the popular open textbook, *The Art of Being Human*, available at anth101.com.

Jiangjiang (JJ) Wu, based in Chicago, is a community health professional at the Chinese American Service League. With a PhD in Anthropology, her current work focuses on community-based research and education, with a particular emphasis on senior health.

www.ingramcontent.com/pod-product-compliance
Lightning Source LLC
Chambersburg PA
CBHW081209130726
47997CB00009B/2609